WILFRED OWEN
WAR POEMS AND OTHERS

WILFRED OWEN

War Poems and Others

Edited with an Introduction and Notes
by

DOMINIC HIBBERD

1973
CHATTO & WINDUS
LONDON

Published by
Chatto & Windus Ltd
42 William IV Street
London WC2N 4DF

★

Clarke, Irwin & Co. Ltd
Toronto

821
OWE

ISBN 0 7011 1989 6

Printed in Great Britain by
T. & A. Constable Ltd
Hopetoun Street
Edinburgh

CONTENTS

5

ACKNOWLEDGEMENTS

Like all who have read and enjoyed Owen, I am much indebted to his editors—Siegfried Sassoon, Edmund Blunden and C. Day Lewis. One doubts whether any poet has had his work preserved and his fame established by three men so distinguished in their own right. The late Mr Harold Owen gave me warm encouragement and Mr Leslie Gunston has been most generous in his assistance. I have not acknowledged all my debts to Owen's critics, but both I and all such critics owe most to Professor D. S. R. Welland, who has put his unrivalled knowledge of the poems at my disposal and showed me much kindness. The staff of the Manuscript Students' Room at the British Museum have been unfailingly civil; I have been grateful for the help and tolerance of librarians in divers places.

Quotations from Owen's letters are from *Wilfred Owen: Collected Letters* edited by Harold Owen and John Bell, by permission of Harold Owen and the Oxford University Press, and the numbering of the letters in that volume is retained here.

My former colleagues at Manchester Grammar School have given me much advice and aid (may the gods smile with special favour upon Richard Cox, Mike Benton and Geoffrey P. Fox), as have some of my former pupils, particularly Graham Holliday. Finally, I must thank Miss Lilian Draper and Mrs Joan Barton for their patient typing from what scholars would, I believe, call 'foul papers'.

J. W. D. H.

FOREWORD

The first collection of Wilfred Owen's poems was edited by Siegfried Sassoon and Edith Sitwell in 1920; it was replaced by Edmund Blunden's edition in 1931, and in 1963 C. Day Lewis produced a third edition which made many improvements upon its predecessors. This fourth edition draws on published sources which have not been available until recent years and it attempts to concentrate into one volume material relevant to an appreciation of Owen's war poetry. All the war poems and fragments are given, with a few minor exceptions, together with a selection from Owen's lyrical and pre-war work chosen to illustrate his style and development. For the first time, the poems are given in an approximately chronological order; an exact sequence has not been attempted, however, since evidence for dating is in some cases still lacking. Extracts from Owen's letters appear among the poems, so that some of the crucial stages in his short life can be understood through his own vigorous words and related to his poetic career. The Introduction is in two parts, the one biographical and the other critical; the Notes provide some facts and comments; the Appendices contain Owen's famous Preface, various additional notes and some suggestions for further reading.

The text of the poems is that established by Mr C. Day Lewis, though a number of minor alterations have been made on the authority of the British Museum manuscripts. A note on the manuscripts will be found in Appendix II. Perhaps as much as half of Owen's surviving verse remains unpublished; it is to be hoped that a fifth edition, both definitive and comprehensive, will eventually be available to the specialist. Much of this unpublished work is undistinguished and unlikely to add to Owen's stature, but even if it does no more than help to free him from that constricting label 'war poet' it will have been worth releasing.

This edition was largely completed before Mr Jon Stallworthy began writing the official biography of Owen. Mr Stallworthy has given a most interesting preview of his book in his 1970 Chatterton Lecture to the British Academy. It is clear that he is going to shed much new light on Owen, demonstrating in particular Owen's debt to the Romantics and his conviction, formed well before the war, that he was destined to be a poet and a messenger.

1893	18 March	Wilfred Edward Salter Owen born at Oswestry.
1895		Mary Owen born.
1897		Owens move to Birkenhead. Harold Owen born.
1900		Colin Owen born.
1901		WO starts at Birkenhead Institute.
1902		
1906-7		Father appointed Assistant Superintendent, G.W.R. and L.N.W.R. Western Region; family moves to Shrewsbury. WO attends Shrewsbury Technical School.
1908		Father takes WO to Brittany for holiday.
1909		Second Brittany visit.
1910		Family moves to Mahim, Monkmoor Road, Shrewsbury.
1911		WO reading Keats's poems.
	Summer	Pupil-teacher at a Shrewsbury Elementary School while preparing for matriculation.
	September	Sits University of London Matriculation exam. Visits British Museum to see Keats MSS. Offered unpaid post as lay assistant and pupil to the Vicar of Dunsden, Oxon. Matriculates without honours.
	20 October	Arrives Dunsden.
1912		Much parish work, including some teaching. Attends classes, in Botany and Old English, at University College, Reading; encouraged by a teacher there to write more poetry and sit for scholarship.
1913	7 February	Leaves Dunsden and rejects evangelical religion. Seriously ill. Harold goes to sea.
	Summer	Sits for and fails the Reading scholarship.
	September	Becomes teacher at the Berlitz School of Languages, Bordeaux.

Poems where date of first composition is fairly certain (*unpublished)	Contemporary events
	Dual Alliance between France and Russia.
	Labour Party founded. Queen Victoria dies. Boer War ends. Liberal victory at polls: social reforms lay foundation of Welfare State. Anglo-Russian agreement. Armed forces strengthened.
Written in a Wood, September 1910.	Edward VII dies.
* *Sonnet: At Teignmouth on a Pilgrimage to Keats's House.* * *Written on a June Night 1911.*	
Various *lyrics, including *The Swift*. Two long *verse tales on themes from Hans Andersen. **On Seeing a Lock of Keats's Hair.*	
January: *On My Songs*.	
Various *sonnets.	

1914	18 March	21st birthday.
	July	Leaves Berlitz to become tutor to a French family, living with them at Bagnères-de-Bigorre, High Pyrenees.
	August	Meets the poet Laurent Tailhade.
	Autumn	Returns to Bordeaux as freelance teacher of English, intending to return to England by Christmas.
	December	Becomes tutor to another family; lives with them at Mérignac, near Bordeaux. Channel unsafe: return home delayed.
1915		
	14 September	Returns to England.
	21 October	Joins up in Artists' Rifles. Meets Harold Monro.
	November	To training camp, Romford, Essex.
1916	4 June	Commissioned as Second Lieutenant into the Manchester Regiment. Training at Witley, Aldershot, Farnborough, Oswestry, Southport.
	30 December	To Base Camp, Étaples, France.
1917	1-2 January	Joins 2nd Manchesters on the Somme near Beaumont Hamel.
	9-16 January	Holds dug-out in No Man's Land (sentry blinded).
	20 January	Into line again. Platoon exposed in severe frost.
	4 February	Sent behind lines for transport course at Abbeville.
	1 March	Rejoins battalion. Concussion after fall into cellar. 2 weeks in Casualty Clearing Station.
	4 April	Rejoins battalion.
	12 April	Successful offensive against Fayet: survives barrage unharmed. No relief for 12 days. Then into quarters at Quivières Fayet.

Poems where date of first composition is fairly certain (*unpublished)	Contemporary events
The Seed.	War. French government moves to Bordeaux. Battle of the Marne. German advance on Paris held. Trench warfare begins.
Various *ballads and other poems.	Gallipoli. German successes on the Eastern Front.
?*Has Your Soul Sipped? To a Comrade in Flanders. Storm. Music* (first draft).	July-November: Somme battles cost both sides over 1 m. casualties. No significant gains. 5 December: Lloyd George becomes P.M.
	Allies reject talk of a compromise peace and state confused war aims.
Happiness (first draft). *Golden Hair.*	
Sonnet to My Friend.	Russian Revolution. Germans deliberately withdraw to Hindenburg Line. U.S.A. enters war.
Le Christianisme.	Allied offensive peters out after slight success. Heavy damage to shipping by U-Boats. Mutinies in French army.

	2 May	To C.C.S. again: shellshock diagnosed. Evacuated by stages to England.
	25 June	Arrives Craiglockhart War Hospital, Edinburgh.
	July-August	Becomes editor of *The Hydra*. Many other activities: meets many local people.
	August	Sassoon arrives at Craiglockhart. WO calls on him *c*. 18 August and again on 21, showing him his poetry and discussing it.
	September	Very active. Some teaching in an Edinburgh school.
	October	Meets Robert Graves
	30 October	Discharged from hospital. 3 weeks' leave, some of it in London. Meets Robert Ross, Arnold Bennett, H. G. Wells, etc.
	24 November	Joins 5th Manchesters at Scarborough for light duties.
	December	Sassoon returns to France. WO promoted to full Lieutenant.
1918	23 January	Attends Graves' wedding in London.
	26 January	*Miners* published in *The Nation*.
	March	To Northern Command Depot, Ripon. Takes a room in a cottage in Borage Lane.
	May	*Song of Songs* published in *The Bookman*. Meets Osbert Sitwell in London.
	4 June	Graded fit for general service. Rejoins Manchesters at Scarborough.
	15 June	*Hospital Barge at Cérisy* and *Futility* published in *The Nation*.

Poems where date of first composition is fairly certain (*unpublished)	Contemporary events
A Sunrise.	
Work on *ballad and Antaeus. The Fates. Song of Songs. Sonnet to a Child. c. 21 August: The Dead-Beat. 30 August: My Shy Hand. The Promisers and Six o'clock in Princes Street written at some time at Craiglockhart.	July-November: 3rd Battle of Ypres (Passchendaele).
The Next War. Anthem for Doomed Youth.	
Disabled. Dulce et Decorum Est. Music (final draft). Soldier's Dream. Winter Song.	
November: Asleep. Apologia pro Poemate Meo.	
Wild with All Regrets. Hospital Barge at Cérisy. ?Conscious.	Russia leaves the war.
Miners February: Last Words.	
Insensibility.	Successful German offensive on the Somme.
April: À Terre. ?The Show.	Further German successes. Haig's 'backs to the wall' order.
The Send-Off. Mental Cases. Arms and the Boy. ?Futility.	
Training.	Germans reach the Marne again and advance on Paris.

13 July	Sassoon wounded and sent home. By the end of the month, WO has decided to return to France.
31 August	To Base Camp, Étaples, again.
September	Rejoins 2nd Manchesters.
29 Sept.-3 Oct.	Successful assault on Beaurevoir-Fonsomme line. Awarded M.C.
29 October	Into the line for the last time.
4 November	Killed in the early hours of the morning in an assault on the Oise-Sambre Canal, near Ors.
11 November	News of his death reaches Shrewsbury.

Poems where date of first composition is fairly certain (*unpublished)	*Contemporary events*
?*The Calls.* 30 July: *The Kind Ghosts.*	
	Allied counter-offensive against over-extended German front.
The Sentry. Smile, smile, smile. Spring Offensive.	Allied advances in Balkans: Germany threatened from South.
	26 September: Allied offensive on Western Front begins. British breach Hindenburg Line. 4 October: Germany sues for peace.
	29 October: German navy mutinies at Kiel. 3 November: Hungary makes peace. Kiel under mutineers' control.
	Armistice: hostilities cease, 11 a.m.

INTRODUCTION

I. OWEN'S LIFE

CHILDHOOD

Wilfred Owen was the eldest of four children. When he was born, his parents were living comfortably with his grandfather in Oswestry; but four years later, on his grandfather's death, the family was forced to move to Birkenhead. Here they lived for ten years in poor districts, struggling against constant financial difficulties to maintain a middle-class style of life. The struggle succeeded well enough at least to cut them off from their rougher neighbours, reinforcing Wilfred's natural liking for introspection and solitude. The family was very tightly knit; yet their relationships were complicated. Mr Owen, who held a responsible but badly paid post with the railways, was a devoted and considerate father, but he was an unhappy man and inclined to intolerance; with his eldest son he had little in common, except music, and they often found it hard to get on with one another.

Wilfred held his mother, however, in adoration; and Susan Owen was devoted to him with a possessiveness that almost excluded the rest of the family. Even from the battlefield he could write, in one of the frequent, long letters which were invariably addressed to her alone, that while other men were fighting for their motherland he was fighting for his mother. It was an exceptionally close relationship, sometimes too close, one feels, to have been really healthy; but Wilfred may well have exaggerated his affection in his adult letters, since Mrs Owen was easily hurt. He was fond, too, of his sister Mary and warmly attached to Colin; Harold, who was nearer his own age than the other two and so more of a threat to his position, was for a long time treated with a patronising disdain that prevented Wilfred even from seeing his brother's talent as an artist until they both grew to understand each other better.

In 1907, the Owens moved to Shrewsbury and conditions improved. Open country was close at hand; from the attic bedroom which he affected, Wilfred could look out across what was then open ground to the Shropshire hills. The Roman ruins of Uriconium were

within easy cycling distance. It was on a family walk through the
buttercup-filled meadows that Wilfred coined the image he later
used in *Spring Offensive*, by describing his brother's boots as 'blessed
with gold'; and on a walk on Caer Caradoc among the bracken,
with his cousin Leslie Gunston, he produced another metaphor
which his cousin used in one of *his* poems:

> Like carven croziers are the curled shoots growing
> To bless me as I pass.

EDUCATION

As a schoolboy, Wilfred was hard-working and contented. His
parents always gave his education highest priority in family affairs
and they expected great things of him—though quite what these
things were, neither he nor they seemed very sure. Occasionally,
Mr Owen would lose patience with Wilfred's bookishness and lack
of interest in more 'boyish' activities; but his wife's determined
championing of her son always overcame his objections. Academic
work for Wilfred was always tremendously important but only
rarely did he see it as an end in itself; his ambitions of scholarship
were based on a stronger and deeper drive, one which it took him
most of his short life to define and bring under control. He did well
at school, though not brilliantly; as soon as he left, he took a job as
a junior teacher in an elementary school and sat, in October 1911,
for the qualifying exam for London University. He passed, though
not, to his grievous disappointment, with honours. His parents were
quite unable to afford fees—if he was to get to university, it had to
be as a Scholar. His mother hoped he would eventually enter the
Church. As a compromise, he accepted an unpaid post as lay
assistant to the Vicar of Dunsden, Oxfordshire, in return for board,
lodging and tuition.

RELIGION

Mrs Owen was by upbringing and conviction an Anglican of the
evangelical school. An evangelical believes that man is saved not
by the good he does but by the faith he has in the redeeming power
of Christ's sacrifice on the cross. Without faith, nurtured by regular
prayer and Bible reading, man is cut off from God. It is important
to be aware of the *sort* of religion Wilfred was brought up in: it
explains much in his poems—the theme of sacrifice, his fondness
for Biblical language, the reality of Hell. A friend of his remembers

how unfailingly regular Wilfred was in daily Bible reading when he was a boy; by 1913 he had rejected much of the orthodox belief of his boyhood, but its influence remained with him.

Mrs Owen's faith was of a fatalistic kind. Everything would turn out all right; if it didn't, there was nothing she could do about it. This, no necessary part of evangelicalism, was part of her character —she required 'self-sacrifice' from her children and insisted, one would guess, that she was sacrificing herself for them; but she suffered from a curious passivity, coupled with indifferent health and a chronic inability to plan ahead. Her children protected her from any painful truth; in return she cared for them and in particular for Wilfred, giving him an inner self-confidence which even the Somme could not break. Nevertheless, Wilfred's attitude to the passivity required by his mother and her religion was an ambivalent one and a recurrent theme in his poetry.

When he went to Dunsden, then, Wilfred was an orthodox evangelical. For a period in the early Shrewsbury days, he had even conducted services at home, dressed in home-made robes before an altar he had built himself. It was a short-lived custom, but it perhaps expressed the close links he already felt between ritual and home, divine and maternal love. It is easy to laugh at this odd ceremony; but a boy brought up in industrial Birkenhead encounters beauty in church more easily than anywhere else. It was in the language of church ritual that Wilfred first began to re-create beauty for himself. If one can imagine the room filled with the scent of flowers, and the glimmer of candle flames reflected in the eyes of his spell-bound family, one can begin to understand the origins of the imagery of a poem such as *Anthem for Doomed Youth*.

As a boy, Wilfred was much given to formal gestures of this sort. Once, on holiday, he heaped masses of wild flowers over his mother as she pretended to sleep. Again, it was a sort of living metaphor, a comparison between flowers, sleep and maternal affection—an almost impersonal statement in the use of imagery.

First Poems

Owen always claimed that he first became aware of his poetic calling before the move to Shrewsbury, on a holiday with his mother in the Cheshire countryside at Broxton. The first of his poems to which a date can be ascribed with any certainty was written some years later when he was seventeen. It may be that he started writing poetry simply as one of his many activities; certainly he showed his poems to his cousin, with whom he also pursued interests in archaeology, botany, astronomy and geology; but in the next few years he became increasingly certain that he wanted to become an artist of some sort. He considered painting, his brother's art, and music, for which he had talent and enthusiasm; but all the time he worked towards finding and shaping his skill as a poet. It *was* a matter of shaping: art, like school work, was for Owen always a matter of hard labour and much revision.

One evening at Dunsden Vicarage, Owen and Leslie Gunston (who lived not far away) listened to the swifts crying round the house; after a while, Owen suggested they should each write a poem on 'The Swift'. From this developed a regular habit of exchanging sonnets on set subjects; at some later stage, the cousins were joined in the enterprise by a friend, Olwen Joergens. Of the poems in this book, at least four were written for this partnership— *Happiness*, *Music*, *The End* and *My Shy Hand*. Owen was two years older than his cousin, but their companionship was a major stimulus to his development as a poet. Their poems were partly cast in a convention that means little to a later generation; but it was by this sort of hard practice that Owen learnt the disciplines of his craft.

DUNSDEN

Dunsden was not a success. None the less, it helped Owen to find his feet. He was expected to work very hard in the parish and he received little of the promised tuition. The Vicar's rigid views and insensitivity to the wretchedness of life in the poorer houses of the area helped to undermine Owen's own faith. Apart from the pleasure of living in the countryside, Owen's main enjoyment came from working with the local children, in Sunday School and on outings; throughout his life, he had a great affection for small children and seems to have attracted them. In his mother's absence, Owen found orthodox Christianity ever less convincing; his dislike of what he later called 'pulpit professionals' began to grow, and a visit to the Keswick Convention strengthened his suspicion that the evangelicals were preaching a pattern of dogma which had little to do with the teaching of Christ. The doctrine that all men were by their natures damned unless they were 'converted' seemed arbitrary and meaningless.

It is possible, too, that Owen's friendships with some of the older village lads became closer than the Vicar might have considered proper. Owen has in some quarters been described as a homosexual, but there is as yet no sound evidence to support such a view. He was certainly late in maturing emotionally and was excessively dominated by his mother; she discouraged him from taking interest in women, a mistake for which he later reproached her. It may well be that the phase of idealistic homosexuality through which many adolescents pass affected him at Dunsden and perhaps continued into later years.

Above all, however, Owen found his understanding of religion to be at odds with his understanding of literature. During 1912 he read a life of Shelley; that poet's conflict with orthodoxy must have impressed him profoundly. If he became an evangelical minister, he felt he would have to abandon poetry, both his own and that of others. He would also have to ignore his knowledge of science in order to accept, and preach, the strict doctrine of the Fall and the consequent nonsense of Darwinism. He was beginning to lead a double life, in public maintaining a respectable religious front and in private writing, under growing emotional pressure, verse of which not a surviving line conforms with orthodox belief and most of which, indeed, makes no mention of formal religion at all.

Owen was faced with the double ordeal of breaking away both from his mother's faith and from the God he had been brought up to worship. A burst of Revivalist fervour in the parish forced him to declare his position; in February 1913 he left the Vicarage and returned to Shrewsbury in a state of sore distress. The serious illness which followed is described by Harold Owen as 'congestion of the lungs' but Wilfred's letters record that its worst symptoms were 'phantasies' or 'horrors', which seems to indicate that his susceptibility to nightmares did not begin with shell-shock in 1917. How Mrs Owen reacted to her son's apostasy is not recorded; perhaps the task of nursing him back to health softened the blow. He was fit again in a few weeks but hopes of a Church career were now ended. Later in the year, he sat a scholarship to Reading University and failed. What he afterwards called 'the B.A. craze' was then over, too; there was not much chance that another try would be either possible or successful.

Being without a degree was not then as serious a bar to progress as it is now; but Owen was forced to recognise that he was to be neither a churchman nor a scholar. The lack of money which plagued the whole family, and which at this time caused Harold to be sent off to sea, prevented Wilfred's settling down to write. Instead, he decided to work abroad and to learn as much as he could of France and French culture. By mid-September he was in Bordeaux, as a teacher of English in the Berlitz School of Languages.

BORDEAUX

The Berlitz School was no fun, either. Teachers were forced to work immensely long hours for an absurdly low wage. Owen was ill again during the winter. 1914, however, brought a change in fortunes: in July he left the School to take up a private tutorship with a friendly and prosperous family. The Légers lived in a delightful villa in the Pyrenees. Here, in sun and refreshing company, Owen found his confidence as a man and began to write again. In August, he encountered his first well-known poet, Laurent Tailhade, and the old man gave him affectionate encouragement.

The outbreak of war was not greeted in France with the enthusiasm Owen would have seen in England. His own reactions to it may be seen in his letters. He was beyond the reach of domestic propaganda and felt no urge to join up nor any strong antipathy towards Germany; nor would he have shared Rupert Brooke's joy at the release from pettiness that fighting seemed to offer. The French Government moved to Bordeaux and there were interesting people to meet. There was also a mild flirtation to be conducted with Mme Léger—though this became, it would appear, a little more serious than Owen had intended and perhaps prompted his rather sudden departure in the autumn. His next job, after a period of freelance work, was a similar one and lasted until August 1915. During all this time, Owen kept talking of coming home but he could not decide what to do when he got there; anyway, the Channel was supposed to be dangerous.

The war had been going for nearly a year before Owen came to the conclusion that he would have to join up. He had considered an extraordinary collection of civilian jobs and had held always to the principle that he, as a future poet, was more useful alive than dead. This may seem a selfish attitude; but for Owen everything by this time was subject to poetry's demands. His eventual decision to enlist was no doubt made when he realised that his poetry was not developing as fast as it might. (He quotes a remark by Vigny: 'If any man despairs of becoming a Poet, let him carry his pack and march in the ranks'.) It was a wise decision and well delayed.

TRAINING

Owen enlisted in the Artists' Rifles on 21st October 1915. There followed fourteen months of training in various parts of England. He took a room for use on London leaves near the Poetry Bookshop, a literary centre run by the poet Harold Monro. Here was more encouragement.

> . . . up comes Monro to my room, with my MSS! So we sit down, and I have the time of my life. For he was 'very struck' with these sonnets. He went over the things in detail and he told me what was fresh and clever, and what was second-hand and banal; and what Keatsian, and what 'modern'.
>
> (Letter 422)

Monro, like Tailhade, had written poems decrying war; Owen never came under the influence of any contemporary established writer who applauded it.

1916 was a breathless, busy year. Very few poems have survived from it. Perhaps some were contained in the sack which Owen instructed his mother to burn at some later stage, but there was little time to write. He was commissioned into the Manchester Regiment in the summer. By the end of the year the pale, delicate and perhaps rather affected Sunday School teacher had become a brown, tough and efficient officer. The physical change was remarkable, but Owen's character did not alter.

BATTLE

Owen was drafted to France in the worst winter of the war. His letters tell his story too well for more than the bones of it to need recording here. It is worth realising that the battle experience on which all his poems about war are based was contained within the space of four months, of which not more than five weeks were actually spent in the line. His first tasks were to hold positions in No Man's Land in the Beaumont Hamel area, ordeals recorded in *The Sentry* and *Exposure*; then he was sent behind the lines for a transport course. In March, he fell into a cellar and spent a couple of weeks in a Casualty Clearing Station with concussion. In April, he took part in a successful attack on the village of Fayet and was in continuous action for twelve days, during which he was blown into the air by a shell and had to spend some days sheltering in a hole near the dismembered remains of a fellow-officer. He came out of this unhurt but with neurasthenia, or shell-shock; was returned to the C.C.S.; and was invalided back by stages to Craiglockhart War Hospital, near Edinburgh.

CRAIGLOCKHART

From the beginning of his four months at Craiglockhart, Owen wrote quantities of poetry. It had always had therapeutic value for him, as a disciplined release from tension, and his doctor wisely encouraged him in the activity. During the transport course, Owen had worked on several of the subjects set by the trio of friends; now he wrote on what was probably another (*Fate*, which became *The Fates*); he also started a very long pseudo-medieval ballad. Dr Brock may have suggested the ballad; certainly he suggested a blank-verse poem on the subject of *Antaeus*. The doctor kept Owen busy in all sorts of other ways, too, putting him in touch with literary circles in Edinburgh and trying to involve him in what would now be called social work. Craiglockhart was an enterprising hospital and was viewed with considerable suspicion by the military authorities (Sassoon has left a picture of it in *Sherston's Progress*).

In July, Owen became editor of, and apparently chief contributor to, the hospital magazine, *The Hydra*; in August he acted in a play. He planned to write a play himself and kept up a voluminous correspondence with his mother; she visited him and stayed with friends, to whose small son Owen wrote two poems. It was a busy time and by day Owen was soon happy and confident again; but at night he was, like most of the patients, the victim of violent nightmares. These 'war dreams' persisted for most of his stay and affected him on occasions for the rest of his life. Remembering war experience (cf. Sassoon's poem on this theme) exposed Owen to the risk of further nightmares; writing about war thus took some courage, which may be one reason why most of the verse written before August has nothing to do with contemporary events, but it was the therapy which Owen most needed.

SASSOON

In the middle of August 1917, Owen introduced himself to Siegfried Sassoon, who had been sent to the hospital by the authorities after he had publicly protested that Britain's aims in the war had now become those of 'aggression and conquest'. Whether Sassoon really was shell-shocked or not is not clear, but to label him as such was an ingenious way of rendering his protest ineffective. Sassoon—tall, handsome and older than Owen—was already a well-known poet and was celebrated in army circles for his daring as an officer; with his quick interest in Owen's poems, he won the younger man's heart completely. He readily admitted later that he did not perceive what order of talent he had encountered, but his encouragement was warm and positive, and the example of his own poetry (Owen had read *The Old Huntsman* collection before calling on him) stimulated his new disciple to an astonishing burst of writing.

Old sonnets, such as *Music*, were reworked and offered for criticism. Sassoon liked some of Owen's lyrics, but his own work demonstrated that war held much more potential as a subject than Owen had so far realised. *My Shy Hand*, written at this time, proved to be the last of the sonnets written to a set lyrical subject; the ballad and *Antaeus* were abandoned. New work imitated Sassoon, at first seizing upon the ironic, colloquial style of his attacks upon the consciences of those civilians who were still in favour of the war. *The Dead-Beat* was Owen's first effort in this vein; but he soon outgrew mere imitation and by September he was writing the first of his mature works, drawing on his old lyrical talent and the lessons learnt from Sassoon to fashion his own style and his own approach to his subject.

In the intervals of working on many poems and of discussing them with Sassoon (who was himself writing the poems soon to be published in his second collection, *Counter-Attack*), Owen kept up his other activities in Edinburgh until he was discharged from hospital in October. Through Sassoon, he had already met Robert Graves; now he went at once to London, armed with an introduction to Robert Ross, man of letters and friend of many writers. Ross made Owen known to a circle of well-known authors and the young poet became, at last and all too briefly, a minor literary figure, although few people had seen his poems. It was an exciting and profitable winter, after a happy autumn. Owen naturally enjoyed being an acquaintance of H. G. Wells, Arnold Bennett and others; the year ended on a note of confidence and hope:

> I go out of this year a Poet, my dear Mother, as which I did not enter it. I am held peer by the Georgians; I am a poet's poet.
> I am started. The tugs have left me; I feel the great swelling of the open sea taking my galleon.   (Letter 578)

Over half a century later, it seems odd that Owen should have been proud to call himself a Georgian, a member of a diverse school of poets which has since been much derided; but the contributors to the contemporary anthology, *Georgian Poetry*, included Graves and Sassoon, who both thought of themselves as Georgians in 1917.

YORKSHIRE

Owen was still only fit for light duties and was posted to Scarborough to take charge of the domestic affairs of a large hotel, then used as a barracks. The knowledge that sooner or later he would be graded fit for General Service could be kept at a distance for the time being. More poems were written. Both Owen and his cousin sent in entries for a poetry competition run by *The Bookman*. In January, *Miners*, written at high speed after a colliery explosion which earned daily newspaper articles for a week or more, was accepted for publication by *The Nation*. By now, Owen was writing as a fully developed poet; half-rhyme became part of his style and not just a pleasing ornament, and the poems of this period are wide-ranging and sure. In March, he was sent to Ripon and, having much free time outside the camp, took a room in a cottage near the river where he could work in peace. In this pleasant retreat, poems begun earlier were heavily revised and new pieces were written. Fresh, though unwelcome, stimulus came from the news from France—the Allies were suffering heavy reverses on the Somme, and ground which Owen himself had fought on a year before was again littered with British casualties. Time was pressing: Owen worked furiously. Plans for publication got under way. In May, he met Osbert Sitwell, who was later to help make him famous. Sitwell's own poetry may have suggested to Owen several semi-allegorical, sometimes Biblical themes, such as those used in *The Parable* and *Arms and the Boy*.

In June, Owen was graded 'G.S.' Through some of his new-found friends, he had the chance of a home posting for the duration; he had planned a cottage for himself and had even started buying furniture for it. On the other hand, he had been conscious at least since the previous December of the pull which the Front exerted on all officers at home. The officer could not forget his responsibility for his men; comradeship in the trenches was a bond so tight (*'bound with war's hard wire'*) that it is nowadays almost beyond our comprehension. It is given expression in many war poems: Robert Nichols' *Comrades* is one of the more easily accessible examples. The officer was responsible for every aspect of his men's welfare; the devotion which he felt for them, and they for him, was one of the hidden strengths of the British army and perhaps the principal reason why its morale lasted better than that of any other army in the war. By

1918, the soldiers were almost more concerned with fighting for each other than for the people at home. Unlike their French and Russian counterparts, the British troops did not mutiny, but home propaganda was wearing thin and civilian demands for total victory. began to cause revulsion at the Front. To intelligent subalterns like Sassoon and Owen, England seemed full of profiteering and jingoistic clap-trap. The gulf between civilians and combatants was so great that people were using the old phrase 'The Two Nations' to describe it. Sassoon recorded his deep unease in *Sick Leave*; as soon as he was fit in December, he had gone back to France, to be with the only people who knew what war was like, and to continue his protest against the war without the risk of being branded a coward.

For Owen, it was once again Sassoon who provided the final stimulus to action. In July, the older poet was sent home with a serious head-wound. In addition to the other reasons for Owen's going out again, there was now the knowledge that there was no one at the Front who would take up Sassoon's task. Owen's letters of this time are filled with a deep sadness based on the certainty of death; his mind was made up at last. By the end of August, farewells were completed, embarkation leave over, and he was in France for the last time. It is quite clear, both from his own letters and from his brother's record, that he did not expect to return. His final words to his mother had been a favourite quotation from Tagore's *Gitanjali*:

> When I go from hence let this be my parting word, that
> what I have seen is unsurpassable.

FRANCE AGAIN

The first few weeks in France were unexpectedly easy. Owen was well behind the lines; he had time, apparently, to re-read Swinburne and plenty of Shelley, and to write. *The Sentry* and perhaps *Exposure* were completed; *Smile, smile, smile* was written quickly for Sassoon. This poem is usually supposed to be Owen's last; he sent it to Sassoon on the 22nd September and the final draft is dated the 23rd. However, the same package included part of *Spring Offensive* and Owen asked if the latter were worth continuing. It seems probable, therefore, that *Spring Offensive* is the later poem and that its final stanza, scribbled in pencil on the back of the manuscript, marks the end of Owen's work.

After the last poem—or at any rate after most of it—came the last fighting. Owen fought with a vigour which earned him the

Military Cross 'for conspicuous gallantry and devotion to duty'. He was left numb but not neurasthenic. He had been actively involved in the worst brutalities of war, by his own choice. There was little time to think, however; a young subaltern could only expect to live for a week or two in the trenches. Owen was killed seven days before the war ended.

The fateful telegram reached Shrewsbury about an hour after the Armistice was signed. In that town, the Abbey Church records the death of the soldier—'Lt. W. E. S. Owen, M.C., Manchester Regiment'—but the poet has no memorial.

II. OWEN'S POEMS

EARLY WORK

In his fragmentary Preface to a volume that was to have contained only poems about war, Owen states firmly that he is 'not concerned with Poetry'—his subject is 'War, and the pity of War'. Up to 1917, his experience had not given him a clear subject; some contemporary thinking did not regard the subject of a poem as particularly important. Artists and critics of the 'Aesthetic' school had claimed that what mattered about a poem was not its meaning but its 'music'— its form, rhythm, mood and inner harmony. The poet should be concerned only with 'Poetry', attempting to capture each moment for itself in its full beauty and intensity. Late Victorian poets delighted in new sounds and in the exquisitely polished handling of difficult forms; often their purpose was no more than to evoke a mood, usually melancholy, and to display their skill.

What survives (unpublished) of Owen's earliest work shows him to have been a competent but not remarkable follower of this convention, learning his craft from Tennyson, Swinburne, Wilde and, above all, Keats. He quickly mastered an impressive variety of stanza forms but their content is of limited interest: there is an ode on *Uriconium* and a quantity of lyrics about sunsets, tears and imaginary lost girl friends. Being a poet was a role which Owen enjoyed. It was easy to find parallels between his own experience and that of the great Romantics; at times he even looked, half-hopefully, for signs of some disease that would bring the early death apparently reserved for those, like Keats and Shelley, 'whom the gods love'.

The reader may decide for himself how much of a poem such as *On My Songs* is fashionable posturing and how much is genuinely felt. Swinburne and Wilde were often poseurs; Keats and Shelley were not, and in the end their influence on Owen was much the stronger. Keats taught him how to use the sounds of words and the shapes of poems, and how to think of himself as a poet, isolated from other men in his search for Beauty and Truth and yet a member of the great fellowship of poets. Shelley, the pacifist and social crusader, whom Owen once called 'the brightest genius of his time', gave him the moral strength of the later poems and the certainty, which Keats only just had time to perceive in his own destiny, that the poet had to work for humanity.

Was it Shelley who gave Owen the strength to break away from Dunsden and endure the awful warnings which the Vicar must have given? Perhaps the Vicar drew Owen's attention to St Jude's ferocious condemnation of heretical and worldly men within the Church who were 'Raging waves of the sea, foaming out their own shame; wandering stars, to whom is reserved the blackness of darkness for ever'. The second half of this verse became the foundation for *O World of many worlds*, in which, clumsily but fervently, Owen welcomes his future as one such meteor in the darkness; the wandering stars are poets and they generate light for themselves, 'rousing men with heavenly fears'. By transposing the image into Shelleyan terms in this way, Owen nicely turned the tables on the angry saint and at the same time produced a poem which curiously foreshadows his later writing. The meteor image, for example, occurs again in *Six o'clock in Princes Street*, where the poet is a messenger pursuing 'gleams' (a word drawn, as Professor Welland shows, from Tennyson's *Merlin and the Gleam*) among 'star-crowds' of poets; and in a letter to Sassoon in November 1917, still looking back to *O World of many worlds*, Owen said:

> . . . you have *fixed* my Life—however short. You did not light me: I was always a mad comet; but you have fixed me. I spun round you a satellite for a month, but I shall swing out soon, a dark star in the orbit where you will blaze.

There is an uncanny accuracy in the strange prophecy of *Storm*, where the poet, in a flash of beauty which is also death, will again make 'men cry aloud and start'. Keats was burnt up, perhaps, by the fervour of his own imagination; Owen was destroyed by war, the same force that brought him poetry and fame, and he became the last of the Romantics to die young.

Few of the early poems have the degree of conviction shown in

Storm. Owen was under no illusions about the amount of practice his craft required and he developed his talent by exercising it, whether he had much to say or not. Consequently many of the minor poems are as obscure as they are elegant; most of them demonstrate his passion for Keats, which became less dominant as he matured though for a time it was intense. *Has Your Soul Sipped?* (C.D.L., p. 112), however, is typical of Wilde and Swinburne in its diction and imagery, as it is in its deliberately shocking—and pretty silly—suggestion that the sweetest of all sweet experiences is to see the smile of a boy who has just had his throat cut. This is indeed Romanticism turned Decadent; yet we should consider the disagreeable possibility that this sort of writing was very good training for a future war poet, particularly the author of *Apologia pro Poemate Meo.* At the same time, the poem is chiefly an exercise in technique; already Owen has discovered pararhyme, a device which is better displayed in *From My Diary, July 1914.*

SOUND

There is no space here for more than a brief digression into Owen's use of sound devices but readers interested in this subject without being well versed in it may find a few simple starting-points helpful.

(i) *Half-rhyme and pararhyme.* There are over forty terms in current use for these two devices and much confusion has resulted. A *full rhyme* occurs when two words are identical in sound from the last stressed vowel onwards, provided that the consonants preceding the vowels are different: *mud/blood, trained/drained.* In a *half-rhyme,* the words are identical only in their final consonant sounds: *bald/old, eyes/close.* The word *pararhyme* was first coined, apparently, by Edmund Blunden in his *Memoir* of Owen, but it was never clearly defined; as used in this book, and in the work of some contemporary critics, the term means a rhyme in which two words are identical in consonant sounds not only after but also *before* different stressed vowel sounds: *leaves/lives, braiding/brooding.* Critics do not always distinguish between half-rhyme and pararhyme. Two further kinds of rhyme, both used often by Owen, are *assonance,* in which words are alike only in their stressed vowel sounds, and *alliteration,* in which words share initial consonants or in which one or more consonants are repeated in close proximity.

Before Owen's first experiments, half-rhyme had occurred often, though never as a regular pattern, in English poetry; pararhyme had been much less common. In a letter at the end of 1917, Robert

Graves, commenting on Owen's recent use of pararhymes in *Wild with All Regrets* (C.D.L., p. 183), pointed out that they are features of ancient Welsh poetry. Owen may have known of this already, since he was aware of his Welsh ancestry and did plan at one time to write verse on 'old Welsh themes'. It is also possible that he knew that the ancient Icelandic poets used half-rhyme, which they called *skothending*. At the beginning of the twentieth century, poets were becoming increasingly dissatisfied with the limitations of full rhyme and many experiments were being tried. Several American writers, notably Emily Dickinson, had broken away from the strict use of full rhyme; in France, Jules Romains began to formulate his complicated system of *accords*, which included pararhyme; in England, Hopkins had discovered, but never used, the Icelandic rhyme schemes; and other poets, despite the horror with which most critics greeted the slightest breach of the rules of full rhyme, were looking for new methods. Robert Graves himself, while still a schoolboy, had written at least one poem partly in half-rhyme. Owen, however, was the first to use either half-rhyme or pararhyme as a consistent rhyme scheme in English. As soon as his poems were published, his remarkable innovation became famous and was widely imitated.

The first recorded evidence of Owen's interest in pararhyme is a list of such rhymes on the back of a draft of *The Imbecile* (C.D.L., p. 139), a minor poem almost certainly written during his first weeks in France in 1913. This gives some support to Professor Welland's suggestion that Owen first encountered the device in the work of Romains; on the other hand, he had learnt a little Welsh even as a child and had studied Old English while at Dunsden, so that he may have discovered enough about ancient literatures to have been aware of the possibilities of partial rhyme before 1913. His first use of half- or pararhyme to describe war was probably in the fragment *Bugles sang*, perhaps written at Craiglockhart; the first complete war poem in pararhyme is *Wild with All Regrets*, revised to become *A Terre*. Sending the poem to Sassoon soon after its composition in December 1917, Owen asked him what he thought of 'my Vowel-rime stunt' as though Sassoon had not seen any examples of it before. (Vowel-rhyme is, of course, an inappropriate term since Owen's rhymes depend upon consonants. In 1918, however, he became friendly with Charles Scott Moncrieff and encouraged him in his translation of *The Song of Roland*. The translation reproduces the original French assonantal or vowel-rhymes and is dedicated to Owen and two others; a draft dedication describes Owen as 'my master in assonance', though Owen himself seems never to have used assonance for a rhyme scheme.) Altogether, half- or pararhyme occurs as a regular pattern in about seventeen poems and fragments; this is a comparatively small proportion of Owen's work, but partial rhymes are, of course, used less systematically in many other poems.

The use of half- and pararhyme to describe war is particularly apt, since they produce an effect of dissonance and failure: we expect the rhyme to be completed and it is not. Owen often makes the second word lower in pitch than the first—*grained/ground, teeth/death* —thereby making the second line sad and heavy. The melancholy effect of this arrangement can be very powerful.

(ii) *Mixed rhyme*. Sometimes Owen used full, half- and pararhyme together in one poem, as in *Futility* or *The Unreturning*. In the latter poem, for example, *world* rhymes with *hurled* but is also a pararhyme with *walled*.

(iii) *Onomatopoeia*. The third and fourth lines of *Anthem for Doomed Youth* are obvious enough examples; more subtle is the clotted, jaw-wrenching language of *Mental Cases* that forces the reader to imitate the twitchings of the madmen.

(iv) *Alliteration and assonance*. Repetition of consonants and repetition of vowels are techniques which Owen developed to a highly sophisticated level. He is particularly fond of the short *u* ('some . . . dull tunnel') in his descriptions of war, but his lyrical passages are full of evocative sounds. The line

Fearfully flashed the sky's mysterious glass

uses tense alliteration (*f, l, s*) and the assonance of the *ea* sound to suggest the nervousness of the men and the sinister menace of the sky.

The wine is gladder there than in gold bowls

has an obvious assonance in 'gold bowls', but there is also a sequence of consonants that is an advanced form of alliteration: *s-g-l-d/g-l-d-s*.

(v) *Internal rhyming*. *The Promisers* (C.D.L., p. 121) has a pair of internal full rhymes in each line. Other poems work to a less formal scheme.

Lifting distressful hands as if to bless

is one of several examples in *Strange Meeting*; there are two pairs here (*Lift/s-if-t* and *-tress/bless*). *The Show* has a pair of some kind in most lines (*long/strung, dithered/upgathered, migrants/mire*). *Anthem for Doomed Youth* has a superb pun on *pallor/pall*, with the further echo of *shall* in the same line.

34

Owen set himself, as most poets do, the task of imposing order upon experience and rendering it beautiful; and because war is a particularly disordered and ugly experience, he needed an unusually highly developed control of words in order to achieve his aim. It must be added that those of his poems in which sound-effects are most conspicuous are not always his best; in a poem such as *Spring Offensive*, he returns to simple full rhyme for the formal pattern and keeps his other devices under such subtle control that they are barely noticeable.

WAR AT A DISTANCE

The first war poems are mostly written in a heavy, conventional rhetoric. *1914* is interesting for its use of Shelley's phrase 'the Winter of the world' and Shakespeare's and Keats's image of autumn; war is seen as the inevitable outcome of previous history and its effect on the arts is of prime concern. The grim optimism of the last line—that out of bloodshed spring will come—is all that Owen contributes to the contemporary conviction that the war was desirable and necessary. *The Unreturning* is one of the first of a number of poems, including *Strange Meeting*, in which Owen considers the next life and finds it unattractive: the passivity of heaven is dreadful, and dawn is, here and elsewhere, not a symbol of hope but a time of fear and death.

It is a common misconception that the shock of war experience forced Owen into sudden poetry. There is in fact no evidence that any of the mature war poems date from before Craiglockhart. Although ideas must have started germinating in the spring, it was the literary shock of meeting Sassoon in August 1917 that made Owen realise clearly how his poetic ambition could be fulfilled. All his major poems were written in the thirteen and a half months which followed. The 1915-1916 period was not very productive; the pieces from the first half of 1917 are mostly sonnets, some written under the arrangement with Leslie Gunston already described.

WAR AND CHRISTIANITY

Without much pretence at chronology, a number of poems about war and Christianity have been grouped together in this edition, because they are the principal body of evidence that Owen was attempting to offer a religious consolation for death in war. Critics— notably Joseph Cohen (*Wilfred Owen's Greater Love*, *Tulane Studies in English*, VI, 1956), who later retracted the views he expressed in this article but not before they had met with agreement from other writers—have seen in these poems a theory of 'greater love', a philosophical explanation of the Christ-like love shown by soldiers as they sacrificed themselves. Many war poets of the time, most of them now forgotten, liked to describe soldiers as Christ-figures, dying that others might live. Owen's poems are certainly full of religious language and allusion, but by 1918 his thinking had gone far beyond such elementary symbolism. It was a consolation often given to bereaved people that their son had died for others, but Owen insisted in his Preface that his poems were 'to this generation in no sense consolatory'.

Gilbert Frankau expressed a simple version of the concept of sacrifice at the end of the last of his war poems, *The Other Side*:

> And if posterity should ask of me
> What high, what base emotions keyed weak flesh
> To face such torments, I would answer: "*You!*
> Not for themselves, O daughters, grandsons, sons,
> Your tortured forebears wrought this miracle;
> Not for themselves, *accomplished utterly*
> This loathliest task of murderous servitude;
> But just because they realized that thus,
> *And only thus*, by sacrifice, might they
> Secure a world worth living in—*for you.*" . . .

Whilst according Frankau's statement the respect it deserves, we may observe that Owen never makes one so clear or so convinced. His first reflections are summed up in letters written before he met Sassoon. Patriotism and religion are incompatible because patriots demand retaliation where Christ preaches 'Passivity at any price' (Letter 512); Christ's command is obeyed only in No Man's Land, where men on both sides lay down their lives for their friends. (Which friends? Does the soldier die for his country or only for his mates in the line?) Owen was not particularly patriotic and was usually very careful not to identify his poems with either side; on the other hand, he was repelled by the prospect of passivity in any form, as his last poems and last fighting demonstrate especially clearly. Sacrifice involves an inactive yielding, which was not a useful quality in the trenches; the image of the soldier as Christ, which Owen admired immensely in Sassoon's *The Redeemer* when he first read it, does not bear too much looking into. One could divide the persons of God the Father and God the Son, and blame the Father for everything aggressive; one could blame the priests and scribes, Church and State. Owen did both on occasions, but as a fighting officer he knew he was as guilty as anybody else of bloodshed. In an obscure passage in Letter 539 (August 1917), he seems to reject the ideal of 'greater love' permanently.

The seventh stanza of *Exposure*, despite its eccentric punctuation and liberal use of *since, for* and *therefore* to suggest a logical sequence that is not really very clear, is the fullest statement in a major poem of the belief that men must die, like Christ, in order that humanity may be purified. In other poems, for example *Inspection*, this belief is satirised. In *Greater Love*, it is given a subjective expression that seems distinctly Decadent (it is frustrating to be unable to date this poem accurately, but it may be early and Owen includes it only under *Doubtful* in his Table of Contents). *The Parable of the Old Man and the Young* may be later, contemporary with the following often-quoted passage from a 1918 letter to Osbert Sitwell, in which Owen describes his men as Christ and himself as crucifier: both the poem and the letter have an unusually laboured quality of metaphor— Owen was perhaps trying to impress his new friend:

> For 14 hours yesterday I was at work—teaching Christ to lift his cross by numbers, and how to adjust his crown; and not to imagine he thirst till after the last halt; I attended his Supper to see that there were no complaints; and inspected his feet to see that they should be worthy of the nails. I see to it that he is dumb and stands to attention before his accusers. With a piece of silver I buy him every day, and with maps I make him familiar with the topography of Golgotha.
>
> (Letter 634)

In so far as the Christ-crucifier image embodies Owen's concern with his position as a 'conscientious objector with a very seared conscience', it is central to his poetry. The religious clothing of the idea, however, does not seem to represent part of any 'theory' about the common soldier as a redeemer of man: such a concept was an early interest of Owen's but he did not pursue it very far. In *Strange Meeting* and *Spring Offensive*, he presents the soldier as the opposite of a messiah, sacrificed indeed but to no purpose, and damned, without hope.

SHELL-SHOCK AND SASSOON

Owen's immediate reaction after his experience in the trenches was to write about anything but that experience. There survives a notebook from his Casualty Clearing Station visits in which he pencilled drafts of *Sonnet to my Friend* and various unpublished poems in the same vein. *Happiness* dates from this period, too, and Owen later considered it to contain his first mature lines—a maturity which, he felt, Tennyson never had and which he himself would not have had either 'but for Beaumont Hamel' (Letter 538). Nevertheless, *Happiness* does not explicitly relate such maturity to his war experience. *The Fates* (C.D.L., p. 122), like *My Shy Hand*, states the creed of Keats's Grecian Urn that only in beauty is there refuge from the ravages of time, an idea which Owen described as 'almost my Gospel'; but here again, beauty is not redefined in the context of war. The doctor at Craiglockhart saw that Owen needed to write, but memories of the trenches found no expression in prescribed subjects and made their way out as nightmares instead.

The contrast between *Song of Songs* and the first draft of *The Dead-Beat*, written within six weeks of one another, is sufficient indication of the effect upon Owen's poetry of his encountering Sassoon. A glance at the war poems in *The Old Huntsman* collection will show how Sassoon's work opened up a new world for Owen: colloquial speech, satire and the harsh retelling of actual experience were some of their characteristics which Owen was quick to imitate. The first draft of *The Dead-Beat* was a rushed and ill-planned piece, built out of re-used and borrowed materials. However, a close comparison between the first and final drafts will show how the poet moved away from his first crude attack upon non-combatants to a recognition that his own hands were far from clean. One may see, too, how he accepted Sassoon's advice about the poem and yet produced a final version which was less like Sassoon's work than the first.

'THE OLD LIE'

> War supplies two opportunities to the poet: he can give articulate voice to the love of country and the love of freedom and any other special idea that animates either combatant, such as respect for a nation's pledged word or the protection of the weak against the strong; and also he can celebrate the heroic exploits of armies and individuals which every war calls forth.

These prefatory remarks by the Dean of Norwich to *Our Glorious Heritage*, a book of patriotic verse for boys and girls hastily published in 1914, seem almost bizarre when set against the poetry of the war that was coming. The Dean, however, is entirely orthodox and many people would still accept his views (which of us, after all, has not found John of Gaunt's great speech impressive?); and he could not foresee the Somme. Sassoon's anger against the makers of the war was simple and strong. 'The old lie' that it was sweet and decorous to die for one's country had to be destroyed at home: civilians had to be told what war was really like. Both he and Owen tend to be best known for their 'shocking' poems; Owen's attempts to upset the civilian stomach are more easily noticed and understood than his other work and some of them are brilliantly handled. His mastery of the final 'punch', evident in some of the early lyrics, comes into its own in poems such as *The Chances* and *S.I.W.*; and in his use of dramatic techniques such as direct speech (including actual quotation), abrupt punctuation and ironic understatement, he quickly rivalled Sassoon.

Few of these poems, however, adopt a preaching tone: more often, Owen involves himself, sometimes at the very end of the poem, or leaves the reader to make up his own mind, closing several poems with a question mark. Those poems that do preach a moral directly at the reader seem less fluent than the rest. The last section of *Dulce et Decorum Est* is excessive and confusing in its unpleasantness: the deep-sea imagery which precedes it embodies Owen's own horror without ulterior motive and its force is correspondingly more lasting.

Although he classified a number of his poems as *Protest*, Owen is not a poet of protest: the war was a human catastrophe and he himself, as a human, an officer and a poet, was part of it. It was this wider sympathy and more accurate self-knowledge that was to make him a much greater poet than Sassoon; but for the moment his task was to absorb his new discoveries and integrate them with the skills he possessed already.

'WHY DON'T THEY COME?'

Most poets of the war took as their subjects the fighters, the dead or the civilians. Owen's style found one of its first fully original expressions in a series of studies of survivors. In *Disabled* and *A Terre*, the elegiac tone is in tension with our knowledge that the men are still alive. All that these men valued in their pre-war life—sex, sport, martial splendour, money, social class—have become the forces that led to mutilation. A man euphemistically classed as 'disabled' is the worst detritus of war, too horrible for most people to look at and yet not dead. The last question of *Disabled* has no general answer; it incriminates no particular section of society but is asked of every man to face as he may.

The blood imagery of 'Disabled' carries the sexual theme of that poem; in *Inspection*, blood is *dirt* to be washed away for the satisfaction of both Lieutenant Owen and 'Field-Marshal God', though not as a useful sacrifice. In *A Terre*, Owen takes up the metaphor of *dirt* in an attempt to describe the 'philosophy of many soldiers' without reference to Christianity. The dying officer, seeing that dirt, or earth, is all he will become, abandons illusions of glory and social superiority and envies the sweep and the muckman, who live with dirt and can handle it. He considers the belief that the soul can move from one creature to another after death, and then tries to relate the Romantic image of 'becoming one with nature' to becoming merely earth; but finally he admits that this is a *poor comfort*. *A Terre* suffers, however, from its clothing of complex ideas in colloquial language, and also perhaps from Owen's lack of grounding in serious philosophical literature: he had neither the kind of training nor the kind of mind needed to make a complete success of a poem of this sort.

In *Conscious*, another poem about a survivor, the strange hallucination seen by the sick man is puzzling at first: 'Music and roses burst through crimson slaughter'. This line, together with the poem's accurate detail, suggests that Owen is—with the advantage of hindsight—describing himself in hospital. The line may record the dawn of his perception that the sounds and sights of battle could be transformed into poetry and made beautiful by metaphor. The desperate short phrases of the last three lines represent not only the patient's effort to gain control of his faculties but also the poet's fear that there will be neither the time nor the illumination to ask in poetry the questions he has not even formulated. It was on this sort of perception, made urgent by this sort of fear that Owen based his finest work.

Adapting the style which he had been developing before August 1917 to the subject of war was not an easy task. In some of the war poems written later in that year lyrical writing appears without seeming sure of its function. Sometimes, indeed, Yeats's celebrated comment that Owen was 'all blood, dirt and sucked sugar stick' seems almost justified.[1] An attempt to write about war in pararhymed couplets came to nothing in the fragment *Bugles sang*, but

---

[1] No attempt is made here to go into Yeats's opinion of Owen, or his influence on him. Two useful articles are: *In Memory of W. B. Yeats—and Wilfred Owen* by Joseph Cohen, in *Journal of English and Germanic Philology*, LVIII, 4, Oct. 1959; and *W. B. Yeats and Wilfred Owen*, by Jon Stallworthy, in *Critical Quarterly*, II, 3, Autumn 1969.

the twilit melancholy of those lines was irresistible; Owen used bits of the fragment in at least three other poems, including *Disabled* and an early draft of *Anthem for Doomed Youth*. Red flowers were experimented with again, in a sketch for a poem on *Beauty*; the Swinburnian possibilities of red and white flowers as images of war were attractive and were to be used, in association with what are recognisably Fatal Women, in such poems as *The Send-Off* and *The Kind Ghosts*. One of the most tempting media for war poems of the kind Owen knew he could write was Tennysonian rhetoric; the temptation is most fully yielded to in *Hospital Barge at Cérisy* but it leaves its trace in many other poems. Tennyson's influence on Owen was by no means entirely harmful, but the parallel between the soldiers in the barge and King Arthur scarcely helps to expose 'the old lie' about war. Owen needed a style which would express the pity of war without substituting disgust for grief, a language which would make it possible to remember the dead 'at the going down of the sun' without concealing the fact that they had been slaughtered 'like cattle'. *Anthem for Doomed Youth*, written as early as September 1917, shows Owen already well on the way towards achieving such a style; the poem, despite its dismissal of formal ceremonies as 'mockeries', is itself a ceremony, a requiem formed out of the sounds of war and the sorrow of bereaved families. Some critics cannot accept this paradox, feeling, perhaps, that all forms of grief and remembrance are only ways of making war less horrible than it is; those who do not share this feeling rank the sonnet among Owen's most successful poems.

Satire aims to stimulate social action, elegy to arouse memory and grief. It did not take Owen long to perceive that his talent was more elegiac than satirical. In December he read a translation of Bion and Moschus, whose elegies were the models for Shelley's *Adonais*; in the summer of 1918 he considered entitling a volume of his poems *With Lightning and with Music*, a phrase from Shelley's great elegy, or *English Elegies*; his Preface refers to all his war poems as 'elegies'. Critics who expect Owen in every poem to try to provoke social action against war are forgetting the function of elegy and making demands on it which are sometimes more political than literary.

'A POET'S POET'

In the winter and early spring of 1917-1918, Owen examined and consolidated his position as a recognised poet who was beginning to break new ground. He drew heavily on his experiences of a year

41

before, perhaps even looking them up in his letters, which he regarded as his only diary. Letter 482, for example, shows how he could turn a personal detail ('I thought of you and Mary without a break all the time') into an image applicable to soldiers in general in *Exposure* ('Slowly our ghosts drag home'). The first six stanzas of *Exposure* are perhaps Owen's finest piece of descriptive writing; they may be part of this winter's revision work.

The 'poet's poet' of this period made two major statements of his role in war. *Apologia pro Poemate Meo* is a personal 'defence' of the subject-matter of his previous poetry; *Insensibility* is an ode on the poetic imagination. In both poems, Owen might be thinking of Shelley's *Defence of Poetry*. Shelley claims that 'Poetry turns all things to loveliness' and that 'it marries exultation and horror'. In *Apologia*, 'exultation' is listed as one of a number of pleasurable elements in fighting, all described in deliberately conventional Romantic language. It is not easy to accept that war can be beautiful. One of the poem's rejected titles was *The Unsaid* and the majority of Owen's previous poems had made explicit only the 'horror' of war. Sassoon's aim was to shock people into action; Owen's was developing into a wider desire to arouse sympathy, so that he had increasingly less use for shock-tactics. Shelley also says that poetry should bring men into sympathy with one another by revealing to them the beauty in each other and in all things. *Insensibility* demonstrates the poetic imagination in action, in the sympathetic account of the unimaginative soldier; his passionless self-control is a desirable quality for the poet, whose task, it is implied, is to awaken those at home to universal sympathy,

> pity and whatever mourns in man
> Before the last sea and the hapless stars.

The task is not to be accomplished by 'tearful fooling' in the manner of Owen's early work, nor by impassioned preaching or attempts to shock aimed at any particular social group. The poet must lay bare the beauty in war and suffering; in doing so, he is carrying out the same task as any tragic poet. It is limiting and misleading to call Owen merely a 'war poet'.

IMAGES OF WAR

The poems of 1918 are written under an impersonal discipline of a high order. Half-rhyme is perfected, imagery handled with sureness, language chosen with precision. Owen's musical ear is apparent everywhere: the resonant consonants of the last stanza of *The Send-Off*, for instance, or the last despairing question of *Futility* are marvellously controlled. The traditional sources of Romantic imagery — nature, weather, flowers, the sun — are freshly exploited.

Owen continued to describe the horrors of war, but the 'poetic' quality of *Mental Cases* or *The Show* is much stronger than might be expected in such gruesome pictures. Indeed, *Mental Cases* is very closely based on an unpublished poem about the damned in hell which almost certainly dates from before Owen's war experience and which is probably influenced by Dante; and *The Show* contains an extended metaphor that would have been the envy of many earlier poets. The comparison in *Mental Cases* of the cycle of night and day to a wound that clots black and breaks open again is horrible description but fine metaphor: there is nothing beautiful in these poems except the poetry.

The development of the extended image is well shown in *Miners*, and there are various small pieces and fragments which are single metaphors no doubt intended for use in longer poems. The network of imagery in Owen's poetry has yet to be fully unravelled. He was fascinated by the cycle of night and day; there are at least ten published and unpublished poems which have a narrative structure based on it (*The Calls* being the only war poem among them) and many of the war poems contain references to dawn, dusk, twilight or darkness. During the war, dawn was the most likely time for an enemy attack; the trench landscape once again became visible; and Owen had always thought of dawn as the hour when, as in *The Unreturning* and *Insensibility*, 'sick men's sighs are drained' and invalids are nearest to death. In the lyrics, dusk is a time for love; in the war poems, it is a time for memory, 'a drawing down of blinds'. Very few war poems are set in sunlight; the sun in *Futility* has given life but cannot restore it, and in *Spring Offensive* the sunlight actually becomes a destructive force. Colours are often symbolic: grey is the colour of dawn, of German uniforms, of deadness; red and crimson indicate warmth, love, blood, sunset, the ecstatic moment of death; darkness may be the twilight of Hell (*Strange Meeting*, *Mental Cases*), an image of the loneliness of the poet or of the desolation of war. Blood is *dirt*, the symbol of guilt equally shared but also the essence of life; it is the sign of sacrifice, to be caught in the shell-hole chalices of the earth, and of the beauty of youth.

Two of the most common subjects in the poems are faces and —

43

surprisingly—laughter. Faces, especially eyes and lips, are mentioned again and again; frequently they are laughing. Sometimes such faces are beautiful and laughing with joy, but in the war poems they are often laughing with the hilarity of 'set-smiling corpses' (*Mental Cases*), like the dead man in *Strange Meeting*, whose 'dead smile' is the clue which tells the poet he is in Hell. The eyes of dying men are particularly terrible and in *Dulce et Decorum Est* and *The Sentry* Owen records that such eyes were a part of his neurasthenic nightmares.

One of Owen's most remarkable achievements is his use of Romantic language in his descriptions of war. Such language, inherited from Keats, Shelley and others, was nearly, if not quite, dead from over-use by 1914; but Owen, in whose work it had always been more vigorous than in the poetry of many of his contemporaries, gave it new life and a highly original twist in his war poems. There is a very close relationship between his wartime and pre-war work, though this is unfortunately almost impossible to demonstrate while so much of his early work remains unpublished. The war poems contain many images more commonly found in love poetry—roses, music, lips and eyes, voices—and pieces such as *Greater Love*, *Apologia pro Poemate Meo* and *The Kind Ghosts* depend for their meaning upon the reader's awareness of Romantic imagery. The line from *Conscious* already quoted, 'Music and roses burst through crimson slaughter', suggests not only the music of *Anthem for Doomed Youth* but also those terrible roses made of torn mouths that the sleeping female (Britannia?) has in her garden in *The Kind Ghosts*. (Several images in Oscar Wilde's poems compare bleeding wounds to red roses.) In his use of nature, too, Owen shows his Romantic lineage: the May landscape of *Spring Offensive* is strongly reminiscent of Keats, but with a difference—instead of creating or enhancing life, nature here destroys it.

The Kind Ghosts is our best documentary evidence of Owen's interest in experiments with sounds: alliteration and internal rhymes are carefully marked on the manuscript and linked together. His comment on *Miners* is worth noting: 'I suppose I am doing in poetry what the advanced composers are doing in music'. *Miners* is not only in half-rhyme: there are also internal echoes, some forming part of the stanza structure (*whispering/wistful, sigh/might*). The whispering sounds at the beginning are followed by the sharp, tormented *i* of *mine, wry, Writhing, I, white;* and these in turn give way to a deep, muted sound that suggests both the depth of the mine and the richness of future centuries, a subtle ambiguity.

44

What further developments of sound and image Owen might have made, one cannot guess. *The Kind Ghosts* was written as he was deciding to return to France. That strange little fragment, *The Roads Also* (C.D.L., p. 96), suggests a new approach to descriptive writing but there is not much else. *The Calls* is little better than doggerel in places. Perhaps, given that his subject was War, Owen needed the stimulus of action. *The Calls* could be taken as evidence that his poetry would have degenerated in peacetime; this depends on how highly one rates the rest of his achievement—and also on what date one gives *The Calls* (the ideas in it could have been in Owen's mind ever since he had been invalided home).

'That sullen hall'

Strange Meeting has been given the place of honour in previous editions and in many anthologies; it has been widely agreed to be, as Sassoon described it, 'Owen's ultimate testament, his passport to immortality, and his elegy for the Unknown Warrior of all nations'. For a long time the general enthusiasm for the poem seemed to prevent its readers from admitting its undeniable obscurity. Apart from including it in his Table of Contents under *Foolishness of War*, Owen has left us with no clues. The final draft has the thirty-ninth line circled in pencil and arrowed to the foot of the page, as though Owen intended this to be the start of a continuation to the poem; the present last line is a hasty addition and was perhaps originally intended to be only temporary. It is possible, therefore, that Owen did not consider the poem to be complete or fit to be shown to anybody else, so it would be unfair to blame him if we find parts of it hard to follow.

Professor Welland has established clear parallels between *Strange Meeting* and Shelley's *The Revolt of Islam*, a poem in which the two principal characters, Laon and Cythna, wage a campaign of non-violence against tyranny. *The Revolt of Islam* is early and very long, a bewildering profusion of prophecy, vision, speech and narrative, but it makes a strong case for pacifism and non-violent resistance; Laon, because he keeps himself guiltless of the crime of fighting, is able to play the reforming role in society that Shelley believed all poets could and should play. There exist several drafts of a poem by Owen in which he seems to be applying Shelley's ideals to a situation such as his own; these drafts are in the form of a speech by the poet to a companion, describing how they will both stand aloof from the evils of war and turn back to beauty and truth, until their wisdom

45

can be used for the cleansing of society. This unfinished poem was revised to become the core of the unknown soldier's speech in *Strange Meeting*.

The rest of *Strange Meeting* has no clear history, but several features of it come also from *The Revolt of Islam*, including the title and the recognition (though the latter, in the form of an encounter with an *alter ego*, is a theme widespread in nineteenth century literature). The description of the cavern in Hell, where the dead sleep and no storms from above are heard, is based, perhaps, on Keats's Cave of Quietude (*Endymion*, IV); the first part of the dead man's speech, with its references to beauty and truth, also looks back to Keats. Recognition in Hell occurs several times in Dante's *Inferno*; the tunnel and its sleeping occupant appear in Sassoon's *Rear-Guard*; and the killing of a friend echoes Wilde's line 'Yet each man kills the thing he loves', which Owen misquotes on a British Museum manuscript. These references to other poets emphasise a point that escaped Sassoon: *Strange Meeting* is not an elegy for the Unknown Warrior but for the Warrior-Poet, and in particular for Wilfred Owen.

In this poem, Owen looks back on the poets who have been his masters and on the lessons he was beginning to learn from them about the messianic task of a poet in society; but he describes not what he *will* do, as in the earlier drafts, but what he *would have* done. Unlike Laon, he is a fighter as well as a poet. The hunt for beauty must be cut short, the truth be left untold. After the war, there will be either complacency or revolution, and a mass retreat from social reform; the poet could have brought right thinking and peace had he lived — but he will not live. Time and death cannot be defied, as they were (in similar language) in *The Fates*; and after death comes only sleep, the passivity Owen had always dreaded.

The pessimism of *Strange Meeting* is deep and unshakeable. There is no suggestion here that death in war is a worthwhile sacrifice; Owen returns to his first attitude to war that the poet is more useful alive than dead The soldier-poet, however, is a killer and he kills a poet who is both his equivalent on the other side and himself. It is this poem, rather than *The Calls*, that should be read as Owen's comment on his decision to return to France.

'LET THIS BE MY PARTING WORD'

Strange Meeting is in many ways a very fine poem, and if we have reservations about its clouded, Biblical language, the oddity of some

46

of its archaic imagery, and its many unexplained lines, we must remember that it may be only a draft of part of a longer work that would have made these things more clear. We must still, however, attempt to understand the nature of 'the wildest beauty in the world', which is not the beauty of women, and 'the truth untold', which is the pity of war. *Strange Meeting* does not explain these phrases, but it was not, as Sassoon appears to have believed, Owen's last poem. The pessimism of *Strange Meeting* raises a further question: If he expected to be killed and thought his death would be useless, why did Owen return to France?

The straightforward answer to this last question has already been suggested: the officer had to be with his men. A special factor, in the case of Owen and Sassoon, was that the poet at the Front could describe the men's sufferings when they had neither the *will* nor the *skill*, as *The Calls* puts it, to do so for themselves. Owen went out, as he says in Letter 662, to 'plead' for his men as well as to 'lead' them, accepting a more limited social duty than the one he outlines and abandons in *Strange Meeting*. He also went out because Sassoon had told him it would be good for his poetry, which makes our judgement of his last poems particularly important. War was good for Owen's poetry partly because it gave him confidence in his standing with civilians (staying in England was, after all, less gallant than winning the M.C.); partly because he could not honestly speak for his men unless he himself shared their sufferings; and partly because war offered an intensity of experience not to be found elsewhere, an 'exultation' that made what one had seen 'unsurpassable' (Owen's quotation from Tagore must not be overlooked).

Yeats's objection to Owen that 'passive suffering is not a theme for poetry' was wide of the mark. Owen wrote about action and returned to action; he was active in pity, in protest and in his hunt for 'the wildest beauty in the world'. There was no beauty or action in wartime England: the hunt led inexorably back to France. This is not an easy truth to grasp. A simpler parallel is the case of the painter, Paul Nash, who said in one of his letters (quoted by Professor Welland) that he wanted to paint in order to show people in England what the trenches were really like; but in other letters, less well known, Nash said that he wanted to paint for painting's sake, because the infernal landscape had a beauty of its own that he could see and was eager to capture. Owen accepted his role as a newsbearer, though he could imagine a higher task for the poet; but he was also driven by his search for intensity (it is Keats's word), the unsurpassable beauty of a moment that is lived to its full and then trapped in art.

'THE IMMINENT LINE OF GRASS'

Owen's last three poems are on one level simple, in accordance with his wish to write nothing 'to which a soldier would say *No Compris*'. *The Sentry* is a blunt description of a personal experience—yet the last line carries greater depths of meaning than are found in any earlier poems of the same kind. *Smile, smile, smile* is a satire in Sassoon's manner—but the survivors have a 'secret' not told to civilians, another aspect of 'the truth untold'. *Spring Offensive* is not easy to compare with any other poem but it too has its secrets and deserves detailed study.

For the content of *Spring Offensive*, Owen went back to his worst war dreams; but he does not mention himself in the poem, making it, unlike *The Sentry*, an impersonal and generalised account. The enemy is not mentioned either and the troops involved are not identified, being referred to only as 'they'. The attack on Fayet was in April but the poem is set in May; this change is particularly interesting because it enables Owen to use his 'blessed with gold' image and to develop the May landscape best loved by English poets. The landscape of the poem is that of home and of literature, compounded of the Shropshire countryside and its buttercups (which are, like long grass, less evident in April) and of the scenery of much poetry, particularly of Keats's Odes (the link is again in the language—*murmurous, oozed*). There may be parallels between this poem too and *The Revolt of Islam*, though this is not the place to examine the evidence; at any rate, *Spring Offensive* and *Strange Meeting* seem to throw light on one another. In both, Owen is 'concerned with Poetry', though not in the sense in which he used the phrase in the Preface: both poems are studies of the relationship between war and poetry and of the intolerable dilemma of the soldier-poet (though *Spring Offensive* is also about every sort of soldier).

Arms and the Boy and other poems had already described the unnaturalness of war. In *Spring Offensive*, as in *Insensibility*, some men are unaware of their situation; they sleep before the attack. Others, however, like the *wise* in *Insensibility*, perceive the implications of war. Contemplating the beauty of the landscape, they are soothed by the drug of summer—'some dull opiate'—in the *body*, but are aware in the *soul* of the menace in 'the imminent line of grass' and in the hard glare of the sky ahead. They stand 'like trees', like part of the landscape and in harmony with it; as they are like plants, so the plants are given human qualities, clinging to the men like the women at home and blessing them with flowers. Nature, in the valley behind where the sun smiles, has tried to prevent war. When the order comes to charge, the men, as it were, uproot themselves; they turn away from the valley to face into the sun, so that its reflection flashes in their eyes. This simple look becomes a heroic gesture; instead of lifting flags and letting them 'flare' in the wind, the men lift their eyes and their eyes flare in the sunlight (in *Anthem for Doomed Youth*, another kind of ceremony had also been replaced by light reflected in eyes). The gesture is a direct challenge and farewell to 'the kind old sun'; its love and bounty are spurned.

Like the poets of *O World of many worlds*, the soldiers have made themselves, for an instant, 'greater than this system's Sun'; but making war is a rejection of the natural order—the offensive is against the Spring as well as in it. The lines race, like the men, up to the sudden, appalling caesura after 'Exposed'. Then nature responds: the landscape of poetry and of home, which the soldier-poet has betrayed, destroys its attackers. The sky burns with fury above, the earth gives way beneath; it is indeed 'the end of the world' and the men fall into the void.

There is no gruesome detail to follow: Owen no longer has any purpose for that. (We may note his use of the word *sheer* in the poem. It twice appears in the letters of this period as 'the only word to qualify my experiences'; it seems an odd choice in the letters until one discovers that some of his nightmares may have been of falling over a precipice.) In his later poems, Owen seems to remember his work before 1917. The prophecy of *Storm* has been fulfilled: the trees have drawn the lightning from the sky and are consumed. The poet has experienced the moment of racing 'exultation' (Owen twice uses this word, too, in his letters, on both occasions to describe his feelings at getting through the barrage at Fayet). After the wild beauty of war, there is a descent into Hell, Owen's last use of a myth that always fascinated him, and the ghastly 'mopping up' operations that followed a successful attack. Some men have survived the sheer fall of the nightmare and they return, but they do not speak their secret knowledge of what has happened to those who do not come back. Do the dead sleep in heaven, 'shaded by the shaking of great wings'; or are they 'under France', lying 'dark for ever under abysmal war'?

And why do the survivors keep silent? As he faces passivity at last, Owen leaves us, typically, with a question.

* * *

Owen said that his poetry might be consolatory to a later generation but that it would not be so to his own. It is certainly true that he did not become widely appreciated until a generation had grown up without the memory of world war. There is no immediate consolation in his poems—except, perhaps, that they were written at all, or that any art could have emerged from the Somme. Owen was not one of those who softened their own consciences by blaming the generals—or the bishops or the civilians or God, or even, indeed, the Germans. He was not a straightforward pacifist, and he has eluded those who have on occasions tried to make him an early herald of socialism or of the protest movement. He is altogether more complex than Sassoon, although he wrote fewer poems and did not often preach. His major poems, the product of one year's writing and twenty-five years' experience, are uneven and sometimes odd; they resist generalisations.

If Owen can be said to have transcended his subject, and to have brought what has often seemed (to him and to us) a grotesque, formless nightmare within the range of the tragic vision, he has given the dead a dignity that will last them better than the ceremonials and fine words with which they have so often been honoured. If, on the other hand, he is only a 'war poet', fettered by his subject and unable to see beyond it; if his pity is indeed, as some have claimed, based on self-pity; at least his craftsmanship is beyond doubt and his poems remain excellent among the ceremonies and music of war. What did English poetry gain from Beaumont Hamel—or lose in the grey dawn on the canal bank at Ors, seven days before the Armistice?

THE POEMS

172. To Susan Owen

4 January 1913   *Dunsden Vicarage*

Murder will out, and I have murdered my false creed. If a true one exists, I shall find it. If not, adieu to the still falser creeds that hold the hearts of nearly all my fellow men . . .

To leave Dunsden will mean a terrible bust-up; but I have no intention of sneaking away by smuggling my reasons down the back-stairs. I will vanish in thunder and lightning, if I go at all.

———————

It has just struck me that one of the occult Powers that Be may have overheard the ancient desire of my heart to be like the immortals, the immortals of earthly Fame, I mean, and is now on a fair way to granting it. This flight of mine from overbearing elders, if it comes off, will only be my version of running away from College (Shelley, Coleridge). Only where in me is the mighty Power of Verse that covered the multitude of their sins. It is true I still find great comfort in scribbling; but lately I am deadening to all poetic impulses, save those due to the pressure of Problems pushing me to seek relief in unstopping my mouth.

Here is a Sonnet that occurred to me this morning:—

On My Songs

Though unseen Poets, many and many a time,
Have answered me as if they knew my woe,
And it might seem have fashioned so their rime
To be my own soul's cry; easing the flow
5 Of my dumb tears with language sweet as sobs,
Yet are there days when all these hoards of thought
Hold nothing for me. Not one verse that throbs
Throbs with my heart, or as my brain is fraught.

'Tis then I voice mine own weird reveries:
10 Low croonings of a motherless child, in gloom
Singing his frightened self to sleep, are these.
One night, if thou shouldst lie in this Sick Room,
Dreading the Dark thou darest not illume,
Listen; my voice may haply lend thee ease.

[O World of many worlds]

O World of many worlds, O life of lives,
    What centre hast thou? Where am I?
O whither is it thy fierce onrush drives?
    Fight I, or drift; or stand; or fly?

5 The loud machinery spins, points work in touch;
    Wheels whirl in systems, zone in zone.
Myself, having sometime moved with such,
    Would strike a centre of mine own.

Lend hand, O Fate, for I am down, am lost!
10   Fainting by violence of the Dance . . .
Ah thanks, I stand — the floor is crossed,
    And I am where but few advance.

I see men far below me where they swarm . . .
    (Haply *above* me — be it so!
15 Does space to compass-points conform,
    And can we say a star stands high or low?)

Not more complex the millions of the stars
    Than are the hearts of mortal brothers;
As far remote as Neptune from small Mars
20   Is one man's nature from another's.

But all hold course unalterably fixed;
   They follow destinies foreplanned:
I envy not these lives their faith unmixed,
   I would not step with such a band.

25 To be a meteor, fast, eccentric, lone,
   Lawless; in passage through all spheres,
Warning the earth of wider ways unknown
   And rousing men with heavenly fears . . .

This is the track reserved for my endeavour;
30   Spanless the erring way I wend.
Blackness of darkness is my meed for ever?
   And barren plunging without end?

O glorious fear! Those other wandering souls
   High burning through that outer bourne
35 Are lights unto themselves. Fair aureoles
   Self-radiated there are worn.

And when in after times those stars return
   And strike once more earth's horizon,
They gather many satellites astern,
40   For they are greater than this system's Sun.

330. To Susan Owen

5 March 1915   *Mérignac*

If I study, it will not be, as writes Father, 'to make a comfortable future'. A comfortable future for myself is to be provided for by other means than study. To some, I seem a fellow without a footing in life. But I have my foothold, bold as any, kept for years. A boy, I guessed that the fullest, largest liveable life was that of a Poet. I know it now; . . . There is one title I prize, one clear call audible, one Sphere where I may influence for Truth, one workshop whence I may send forth Beauty, one mode of living entirely congenial to me . . .

. . . to be able to write as I know how to, study is necessary: a period of study, then of intercourse with kindred spirits, then of isolation. My heart is ready, but my brain unprepared, and my hand untrained. And all,—untested. I quite envisage possibility of non-success.

Storm

His face was charged with beauty as a cloud
  With glimmering lightning. When it shadowed me
  I shook, and was uneasy as a tree
That draws the brilliant danger, tremulous, bowed.

5 So must I tempt that face to loose its lightning.
  Great gods, whose beauty is death, will laugh above,
  Who made his beauty lovelier than love.
I shall be bright with their unearthly brightening.

And happier were it if my sap consume;
10 Glorious will shine the opening of my heart;
The land shall freshen that was under gloom;
What matter if all men cry aloud and start,
And women hide bleak faces in their shawl,
At those hilarious thunders of my fall?

Music

I have been urged by earnest violins
  And drunk their mellow sorrows to the slake
Of all my sorrows and my thirsting sins.
  My heart has beaten for a brave drum's sake.
5 Huge chords have wrought me mighty: I have hurled
  Thuds of gods' thunder. And with old winds pondered
Over the curse of this chaotic world, —
  With low lost winds that maundered as they wandered.

I have been gay with trivial fifes that laugh;
10 And songs more sweet than possible things are sweet;
And gongs, and oboes. Yet I guessed not half
Life's symphony till I had made hearts beat,
And touched Love's body into trembling cries,
And blown my love's lips into laughs and sighs.

Maundy Thursday

Between the brown hands of a server-lad
The silver cross was offered to be kissed.
The men came up, lugubrious, but not sad,
And knelt reluctantly, half-prejudiced.
5 (And kissing, kissed the emblem of a creed.)
Then mourning women knelt; meek mouths they had,
(And kissed the Body of the Christ indeed.)
Young children came, with eager lips and glad.
(These kissed a silver doll, immensely bright.)
10 Then I, too, knelt before that acolyte.
Above the crucifix I bent my head:
The Christ was thin, and cold, and very dead:
And yet I bowed, yea, kissed—my lips did cling.
(I kissed the warm live hand that held the thing.)

[Shadwell Stair]

I am the ghost of Shadwell Stair.
    Along the wharves by the water-house,
    And through the cavernous slaughter-house,
I am the shadow that walks there.

5 Yet I have flesh both firm and cool,
    And eyes tumultuous as the gems
    Of moons and lamps in the full Thames
When dusk sails wavering down the pool.

Shuddering the purple street-arc burns
10   Where I watch always; from the banks
    Dolorously the shipping clanks
And after me a strange tide turns.

I walk till the stars of London wane
    And dawn creeps up the Shadwell Stair.
15   But when the crowing syrens blare
I with another ghost am lain.

From My Diary, July 1914

Leaves
   Murmuring by myriads in the shimmering trees.
Lives
   Wakening with wonder in the Pyrenees.
5 Birds
   Cheerily chirping in the early day.
Bards
   Singing of summer, scything thro' the hay.
Bees
10   Shaking the heavy dews from bloom and frond.
 Boys
   Bursting the surface of the ebony pond.
Flashes
   Of swimmers carving thro' the sparkling cold.
15 Fleshes
   Gleaming with wetness to the morning gold.
A mead
   Bordered about with warbling water brooks.
A maid
20   Laughing the love-laugh with me; proud of looks.
The heat
   Throbbing between the upland and the peak.
Her heart
   Quivering with passion to my pressèd cheek.
25 Braiding
   Of floating flames across the mountain brow.
Brooding
   Of stillness; and a sighing of the bough.
Stirs
30   Of leaflets in the gloom; soft petal-showers;
Stars
   Expanding with the starr'd nocturnal flowers.

278. To Susan Owen

1 August 1914   *Bagnères-de-Bigorre*

The news of War made great stir in Bagnères. Women were weep-
ing all about; work was suspended. Nearly all the men have already
departed. Our household is one in a thousand. Mr. Léger, who
doesn't look his age, and I, who look French, are objects of mark at
present. I had to declare myself, and get a permit to remain here;
where I must stay still under penalty of arrest and sentence as a spy—
unless I get a special visa for emigrating . . . Our food is already much
dearer, and we are all getting ready to live on bread and maize-soup.
If need be, Monsieur & I will undertake the harvest between us.
Nobody is very gay.

285. To Susan Owen

28 August 1914   *Bagnères-de-Bigorre*

The war affects me less than it ought. But I can do no service to
anybody by agitating for news or making dole over the slaughter.
On the contrary I adopt the perfect English custom of dealing with
an offender: a Frenchman duels with him: an Englishman ignores
him. I feel my own life all the more precious and more dear in the
presence of this deflowering of Europe. While it is true that the guns
will effect a little useful weeding, I am furious with chagrin to think
that the Minds which were to have excelled the civilization of ten
thousand years, are being annihilated—and bodies, the product of
aeons of Natural Selection, melted down to pay for political statues.

302. To Susan Owen

2 December 1914   *Bordeaux*

The *Daily Mail* speaks very movingly about the 'duties shirked'
by English young men. I suffer a good deal of shame. But while
those ten thousand lusty louts go on playing football I shall go on
playing with my little axiom:—that my life is worth more than my
death to Englishmen.

Do you know what would hold me together on a battlefield?: The
sense that I was perpetuating the language in which Keats and the
rest of them wrote! I do not know in what else England is greatly
superior, or dearer to me, than another land and people.

1914

War broke: and now the Winter of the world
With perishing great darkness closes in.
The foul tornado, centred at Berlin,
Is over all the width of Europe whirled,
5 Rending the sails of progress. Rent or furled
Are all Art's ensigns. Verse wails. Now begin
Famines of thought and feeling. Love's wine's thin.
The grain of human Autumn rots, down-hurled.

For after Spring had bloomed in early Greece,
10 And Summer blazed her glory out with Rome,
An Autumn softly fell, a harvest home,
A slow grand age, and rich with all increase.
But now, for us, wild Winter, and the need
Of sowings for new Spring, and blood for seed.

The Unreturning

Suddenly night crushed out the day and hurled
Her remnants over cloud-peaks, thunder-walled.
Then fell a stillness such as harks appalled
When far-gone dead return upon the world.

5 There watched I for the Dead; but no ghost woke.
Each one whom Life exiled I named and called.
But they were all too far, or dumbed, or thralled,
And never one fared back to me or spoke.

Then peered the indefinite unshapen dawn
10 With vacant gloaming, sad as half-lit minds,
The weak-limned hour when sick men's sighs are drained.
And while I wondered on their being withdrawn,
Gagged by the smothering Wing which none unbinds,
I dreaded even a heaven with doors so chained.

368. To Leslie Gunston

25 July 1915   *Bordeaux*

You say you 'hear of wars and rumours of wars'. *Vous en êtes là seulement?* You hear Rumours? The rumours, over here, make the ears of the gunners bleed. . . . I don't imagine that the German War will be affected by my joining in, but I know my own future Peace will be. I wonder that you don't ply me with this argument: that Keats remained absolutely indifferent to Waterloo and all that commotion. Well, I have passed a year of fine-contemptuous nonchalance: but having now some increase of physical strength I feel proportionately useful and proportionately lacking in sense if I don't use it in the best way—The Only Way.

388. To Susan Owen

2 November 1915   *Tavistock Square*

If only this Life went on indefinitely I should be well pleased. It is really no great strain to strut round the gardens of a West-end square for six or seven hours a day. Walking abroad, one is the admiration of all little boys, and meets an approving glance from every eye of eld. I sometimes amuse myself by sternly contemplating the civilian dress of apparent Slackers. They return a shifty enough expression.

426. To Susan Owen

2 April 1916   *Y.M.C.A. Romford*

Bugles are now sounded at the proper times. We have also our Drum & Fife Band as well as the Regimental. A thrilling affair. The sound, together with the gallant bearing of the twenty fifers, has finally dazzled me with Military Glory.

The fifers are worthy to rank with the demented violins that make Queen's Hall to spin round as a top, and with the Cathedral Choir that pierces thro' the heights of heaven. Sweetly sing the fifes as it were great charmed birds in Arabian forests. And the drums pulse fearfully-voluptuously, as great hearts in death.

475. To Susan Owen

1 January 1917 France

This morning I was hit! We were bombing and a fragment from somewhere hit my thumb knuckle. I coaxed out 1 drop of blood. Alas! no more!!

There is a fine heroic feeling about being in France, and I am in perfect spirits. A tinge of excitement is about me, but excitement is always necessary to my happiness.

I don't think it is the real front I'm going to.

478. To Susan Owen

9 January 1917 2nd Manchester Regt., B.E.F.

My own dear Mother,

I forget both the day and the date. It is about the 9th. We moved further up yesterday, most of the way on 'Buses.

I have just had your long-looked-for letter. It seems wrong that even your dear handwriting should come into such a Gehenna as this. There is a terrific Strafe on. Our artillery are doing a 48 hours bombardment.

At night it is like a stupendous thunderstorm, for the flashes are quite as bright as lightning.

When we arrived at this deserted Village last night, there had been no billets prepared for the Battalion—owing to misunderstanding. Imagine the confusion!

For my part I discovered, or rather my new chosen and faithful Servant discovered a fine little hut, with a chair in it! A four-legged chair! The Roof is waterproof, and there is a Stove. There is only one slight disadvantage: there is a Howitzer just 70 or 80 yards away, firing over the top every minute or so. I can't tell you how glad I am you got me the ear-defenders. I have to wear them at night. Every time No. 2 (the nearest gun) fires, all my pharmacopoeia, all my boots, candle, and nerves take a smart jump upwards. This phenomena is immediately followed by a fine rain of particles from the roof. I keep blowing them off the page.

From time to time the Village is shelled but just now nothing is coming over. Anyhow there is a good cellar close to . . .

I chose to spend an hour today behind the guns (to get used to them). The Major commanding the battery was very pleasant indeed. He took me to his H.Q. and gave me a book of Poems to read as if it were the natural thing to do!!

But all night I shall be hearing the fellow's voice:
Number Two—FIRE!

Sonnet

ON SEEING A PIECE OF OUR HEAVY ARTILLERY
BROUGHT INTO ACTION

Be slowly lifted up, thou long black arm,
Great gun towering towards Heaven, about to curse;
Sway steep against them, and for years rehearse
Huge imprecations like a blasting charm!
5 Reach at that Arrogance which needs thy harm,
And beat it down before its sins grow worse.
Spend our resentment, cannon,—yea, disburse
Our gold in shapes of flame, our breaths in storm.

Yet, for men's sakes whom thy vast malison
10 Must wither innocent of enmity,
Be not withdrawn, dark arm, thy spoilure done,
Safe to the bosom of our prosperity.
But when thy spell be cast complete and whole,
May God curse thee, and cut thee from our soul!

480. To Susan Owen

16 January 1917   *2nd Manchester Regt., B.E.F.*

I can see no excuse for deceiving you about these last 4 days. I have suffered seventh hell.

I have not been at the front.

I have been in front of it.

I held an advanced post, that is, a 'dug-out' in the middle of No Man's Land.

We had a march of 3 miles over shelled road then nearly 3 along a flooded trench. After that we came to where the trenches had been blown flat out and had to go over the top. It was of course dark, too dark, and the ground was not mud, not sloppy mud, but an octopus of sucking clay, 3, 4, and 5 feet deep, relieved only by craters full of water. Men have been known to drown in them. Many stuck in the mud & only got on by leaving their waders, equipment, and in some cases their clothes.

High explosives were dropping all around out[side], and machine guns spluttered every few minutes. But it was so dark that even the German flares did not reveal us.

Three quarters dead, I mean each of us ¾ dead, we reached the dug-out, and relieved the wretches therein. I then had to go forth and find another dug-out for a still more advanced post where I left 18 bombers. I was responsible for other posts on the left but there was a junior officer in charge.

My dug-out held 25 men tightly packed. Water filled it to a depth of 1 or 2 feet, leaving say 4 feet of air.

One entrance had been blown in & blocked.

So far, the other remained.

The Germans knew we were staying there and decided we shouldn't.

Those fifty hours were the agony of my happy life.

Every ten minutes on Sunday afternoon seemed an hour.

I nearly broke down and let myself drown in the water that was now slowly rising above my knees.

Towards 6 o'clock, when, I suppose, you would be going to church, the shelling grew less intense and less accurate: so that I was mercifully helped to do my duty and crawl, wade, climb and flounder over No Man's Land to visit my other post. It took me half an hour to move about 150 yards.

I was chiefly annoyed by our own machine guns from behind. The seeng-seeng-seeng of the bullets reminded me of Mary's canary. On the whole I can support the canary better.

In the Platoon on my left the sentries over the dug-out were blown to nothing . . . I kept my own sentries half way down the stairs during the more terrific bombardment. In spite of this one lad was blown down and, I am afraid, blinded.

This was my only casualty.

19 January 1917   *2nd Manchester Regt., B.E.F.*

They want to call No Man's Land 'England' because we keep supremacy there.

It is like the eternal place of gnashing of teeth; the Slough of Despond could be contained in one of its crater-holes; the fires of Sodom and Gomorrah could not light a candle to it—to find the way to Babylon the Fallen.

It is pock-marked like a body of foulest disease and its odour is the breath of cancer.

I have not seen any dead. I have done worse. In the dank air I have perceived it, and in the darkness, felt. Those 'Somme Pictures' are the laughing stock of the army—like the trenches on exhibition in Kensington.

No Man's Land under snow is like the face of the moon chaotic, crater-ridden, uninhabitable, awful, the abode of madness.

To call it 'England'!

I would as soon call my House(!) Krupp Villa, or my child Chlorina-Phosgena.

Now I have let myself tell you more facts than I should, in the exuberance of having already done 'a Bit'. It is done, and we are all going still farther back for a long time. A long time. The people of England needn't hope. They must agitate. But they are not yet agitated even. Let them imagine 50 strong men trembling as with ague for 50 hours!

4 February 1917   *Advanced Horse Transport Depot*

I have no mind to describe all the horrors of this last Tour. But it was almost wusser than the first, because in this place my Platoon had no Dug-Outs, but had to lie in the snow under the deadly wind. By day it was impossible to stand up or even crawl about because we were behind only a little ridge screening us from the Bosches' periscope.

We had 5 Tommy's cookers between the Platoon, but they did not suffice to melt the ice in the water-cans. So we suffered cruelly from thirst.

The marvel is that we did not all die of cold. As a matter of fact, only one of my party actually froze to death before he could be got back, but I am not able to tell how many have ended in hospital. I had no real casualties from shelling, though for 10 minutes every hour whizz-bangs fell a few yards short of us. Showers of soil rained on us, but no fragments of shell could find us.

I had lost my gloves in a dug-out, but I found 1 mitten on the Field; I had my Trench Coat (without lining but with a Jerkin underneath.) My feet ached until they could ache no more, and so they temporarily died. I was kept warm by the ardour of Life within me. I forgot hunger in the hunger for Life. The intensity of your Love reached me and kept me living. I thought of you and Mary without a break all the time. I cannot say I felt any fear. We were all half-crazed by the buffetting of the High Explosives. I think the most unpleasant reflection that weighed on me was the impossibility of getting back any wounded, a total impossibility all day, and fright-fully difficult by night.

We were marooned on a frozen desert.

There is not a sign of life on the horizon and a thousand signs of death.

Not a blade of grass, not an insect; once or twice a day the shadow of a big hawk, scenting carrion.

*   *   *

I suppose I can endure cold, and fatigue, and the face-to-face death, as well as another; but extra for me there is the universal pervasion of Ugliness. Hideous landscapes, vile noises, foul language and nothing but foul, even from one's own mouth (for all are devil ridden), everything unnatural, broken, blasted; the distortion of the dead, whose unburiable bodies sit outside the dug-outs all day, all night, the most execrable sights on earth. In poetry we call them the most glorious. But to sit with them all day, all night . . . and a week later to come back and find them still sitting there, in motionless groups, THAT is what saps the 'soldierly spirit' . . .

25 April 1917   *A. Coy., My Cellar*

Immediately after I sent my last letter, more than a fortnight ago, we were rushed up into the Line. Twice in one day we went over the top, gaining both our objectives. Our A Company led the Attack, and of course lost a certain number of men. I had some extraordinary escapes from shells & bullets. Fortunately there was no bayonet work, since the Hun ran before we got up to his trench. You will find mention of our fight in the Communiqué; the place happens to be the very village [Fayet] which Father named in his last letter! Never before has the Battalion encountered such intense shelling as rained on us as we advanced in the open. The Colonel sent round this message the next day: 'I was filled with admiration at the conduct of the Battalion under the heavy shell-fire . . . The leadership of officers was excellent, and the conduct of the men beyond praise.' The reward we got for all this was to remain in the Line 12 days. For twelve days I did not wash my face, nor take off my boots, nor sleep a deep sleep. For twelve days we lay in holes, where at any moment a shell might put us out. I think the worst incident was one wet night when we lay up against a railway embankment. A big shell lit on the top of the bank, just 2 yards from my head. Before I awoke, I was blown in the air right away from the bank! I passed most of the following days in a railway Cutting, in a hole just big enough to lie in, and covered with corrugated iron. My brother officer of B Coy, 2/Lt Gaukroger lay opposite in a similar hole. But he was covered with earth, and no relief will ever relieve him, nor will his Rest be a 9 days-Rest. I think that the terribly long time we stayed unrelieved was unavoidable; yet it makes us feel bitterly towards those in England who might relieve us, and will not.

510. To Colin Owen

14 May 1917   *13th Casualty Clearing Station*

The sensations of going over the top are about as exhilarating as those dreams of falling over a precipice, when you see the rocks at the bottom surging up to you. I woke up without being squashed. Some didn't. There was an extraordinary exultation in the act of slowly walking forward, showing ourselves openly.

There was no bugle and no drum for which I was very sorry. I kept up a kind of chanting sing-song: Keep the Line straight!

Not so fast on the left!
Steady on the Left!
Not so fast!

Then we were caught in a Tornado of Shells. The various 'waves' were all broken up and we carried on like a crowd moving off a cricket-field. When I looked back and saw the ground all crawling and wormy with wounded bodies, I felt no horror at all but only an immense exultation at having got through the Barrage. We were more than an hour moving over the open and by the time we came to the German Trench every Bosche had fled. But a party of them had remained lying low in a wood close behind us, and they gave us a very bad time for the next four hours.

Happiness

Ever again to breathe pure happiness,
The happiness our mother gave us, boys?
To smile at nothings, needing no caress?
Have we not laughed too often since with joys?
5 Have we not wrought too sick and sorrowful wrongs
For her hands' pardoning? The sun may cleanse,
And time, and starlight. Life will sing sweet songs,
And gods will show us pleasures more than men's.

Yet heaven looks smaller than the old doll's-home,
10 No nestling place is left in bluebell bloom,
And the wide arms of trees have lost their scope.
The former happiness is unreturning:
Boys' griefs are not so grievous as youth's yearning,
Boys have no sadness sadder than our hope.

Alternative draft of the sestet:

But the old Happiness is unreturning.
10 Boy's griefs are not so grievous as youth's yearning,
Boys have no sadness sadder than our hope.
We who have seen the gods' kaleidoscope,
And played with human passions for our toys,
We know men suffer chiefly by their joys.

66

Sonnet to my Friend

WITH AN IDENTITY DISC

If ever I had dreamed of my dead name
High in the heart of London, unsurpassed
By Time for ever, and the Fugitive, Fame,
There seeking a long sanctuary at last,—

5 Or if I onetime hoped to hide its shame,
—Shame of success, and sorrow of defeats,—
Under those holy cypresses, the same
That shade always the quiet place of Keats,

Now rather thank I God there is no risk
10 Of gravers scoring it with florid screed.
Let my inscription be this soldier's disc.
Wear it, sweet friend. Inscribe no date nor deed.
But may thy heart-beat kiss it, night and day,
Until the name grow blurred and fade away.

The End

After the blast of lightning from the east,
The flourish of loud clouds, the Chariot Throne;
After the drums of time have rolled and ceased,
And by the bronze west long retreat is blown,

5 Shall Life renew these bodies? Of a truth,
All death will he annul, all tears assuage?—
Or fill these void veins full again with youth,
And wash, with an immortal water, age?

When I do ask white Age, he saith not so:
10 'My head hangs weighed with snow.'
And when I hearken to the Earth, she saith:
'My fiery heart shrinks, aching. It is death
Mine ancient scars shall not be glorified,
Nor my titanic tears, the seas, be dried.'

Already I have comprehended a light which will never filter into the dogma of any national church: namely that one of Christ's essential commands was: Passivity at any price! Suffer dishonour and disgrace; but never resort to arms. Be bullied, be outraged, be killed; but do not kill. It may be a chimerical and an ignominious principle, but there it is. It can only be ignored: and I think pulpit professionals are ignoring it very skilfully and successfully indeed.

Have you seen what ridiculous figures Frederick and Arthur Wood [two contemporary evangelists] are cutting? If they made the Great Objection, I should admire them. They have not the courage.

. . . But I must not malign these Brethren because I do not know their exact Apologia.

And am I not myself a conscientious objector with a very seared conscience?

. . . Christ is literally in no man's land. There men often hear His voice: Greater love hath no man than this, that a man lay down his life—for a friend.

Is it spoken in English only and French?

I do not believe so.

Thus you see how pure Christianity will not fit in with pure patriotism.

Greater Love

Red lips are not so red
   As the stained stones kissed by the English dead.
Kindness of wooed and wooer
Seems shame to their love pure.
5 O Love, your eyes lose lure
   When I behold eyes blinded in my stead!

Your slender attitude
   Trembles not exquisite like limbs knife-skewed,
Rolling and rolling there
10 Where God seems not to care;
   Till the fierce love they bear
   Cramps them in death's extreme decrepitude.

Your voice sings not so soft,—
　　Though even as wind murmuring through raftered loft,—
15 Your dear voice is not dear,
　　Gentle, and evening clear,
　　As theirs whom none now hear,
　　　Now earth has stopped their piteous mouths that coughed.

　　Heart, you were never hot
20 　Nor large, nor full like hearts made great with shot;
　　And though your hand be pale,
　　Paler are all which trail
　　Your cross through flame and hail:
　　　Weep, you may weep, for you may touch them not.

The Parable of the Old Man
and the Young

　　So Abram rose, and clave the wood, and went,
　　And took the fire with him, and a knife.
　　And as they sojourned both of them together,
　　Isaac the first-born spake and said, My Father,
5 Behold the preparations, fire and iron,
　　But where the lamb for this burnt-offering?
　　Then Abram bound the youth with belts and straps,
　　And builded parapets and trenches there,
　　And stretchèd forth the knife to slay his son.
10 When lo! an angel called him out of heaven,
　　Saying, Lay not thy hand upon the lad,
　　Neither do anything to him. Behold,
　　A ram, caught in a thicket by its horns;
　　Offer the Ram of Pride instead of him.

15 But the old man would not so, but slew his son,
　　And half the seed of Europe, one by one.

Le Christianisme

So the church Christ was hit and buried
    Under its rubbish and its rubble.
In cellars, packed-up saints lie serried,
    Well out of hearing of our trouble.

5 One Virgin still immaculate
    Smiles on for war to flatter her.
She's halo'd with an old tin hat,
    But a piece of hell will batter her.

At a Calvary near the Ancre

One ever hangs where shelled roads part.
    In this war He too lost a limb,
But His disciples hide apart;
    And now the Soldiers bear with Him.

5 Near Golgotha strolls many a priest,
    And in their faces there is pride
That they were flesh-marked by the Beast
    By whom the gentle Christ's denied.

The scribes on all the people shove
10   And brawl allegiance to the state,
But they who love the greater love
    Lay down their life; they do not hate.

538. To Susan Owen

8 August 1917   *Craiglockhart*

At present I am a sick man in hospital, by night; a poet, for a quarter of an hour after breakfast; I am whatever and whoever I see while going down to Edinburgh on the tram: greengrocer, policeman, shopping lady, errand boy, paper-boy, blind man, crippled

Tommy, bank-clerk, carter, all of these in half an hour; . . . then I either peer over bookstalls in back-streets, or do a bit of a dash down Princes Street,—according as I have taken weak tea or strong coffee for breakfast.

Six o'clock in Princes Street

In twos and threes, they have not far to roam,
   Crowds that thread eastward, gay of eyes;
Those seek no further than their quiet home,
   Wives, walking westward, slow and wise.

5 Neither should I go fooling over clouds,
   Following gleams unsafe, untrue,
And tiring after beauty through star-crowds,
   Dared I go side by side with you;

Or be you in the gutter where you stand,
10   Pale rain-flawed phantom of the place,
With news of all the nations in your hand,
   And all their sorrows in your face.

[Antaeus: a fragment]

So neck to stubborn neck, and obstinate knee to knee,
Wrestled those two; and peerless Heracles
Could not prevail, nor get at any vantage . . .
So those huge hands that, small, had snapped great snakes,
5 Let slip the writhing of Antaeus' wrists:
Those hero's hands that wrenched the necks of bulls,
Now fumbled round the slim Antaeus' limbs,
Baffled. Then anger swelled in Heracles,
And terribly he grappled broader arms,
10 And yet more firmly fixed his graspéd feet.
And up his back the muscles bulged and shone
Like climbing banks and domes of towering cloud.
And they who watched that wrestling say he laughed,
But not so loud as on Eurystheus of old.

71

Song of Songs

Sing me at morn but only with your laugh;
Even as Spring that laugheth into leaf;
Even as Love that laugheth after Life.

Sing me but only with your speech all day,
5 As voluble leaflets do; let viols die;
The least word of your lips is melody!

Sing me at eve but only with your sigh!
Like lifting seas it solaceth; breathe so,
Slowly and low, the sense that no songs say.

10 Sing me at midnight with your murmurous heart!
Let youth's immortal-moaning chords be heard
Throbbing through you, and sobbing, unsubdued.

My Shy Hand

My shy hand shades a hermitage apart,—
 O large enough for thee, and thy brief hours.
Life there is sweeter held than in God's heart,
 Stiller than in the heavens of hollow flowers.

5 The wine is gladder there than in gold bowls.
 And Time shall not drain thence, nor trouble spill.
Sources between my fingers feed all souls,
 Where thou mayest cool thy lips, and draw thy fill.

Five cushions hath my hand, for reveries;
10 And one deep pillow for thy brow's fatigues;
Languor of June all winterlong, and ease
 For ever from the vain untravelled leagues.

Thither your years may gather in from storm,
And Love, that sleepeth there, will keep thee warm.

22 August 1917   *Craiglockhart*

My dear Leslie,

   At last I have an event worth a letter. I have beknown myself to
Siegfried Sassoon. Went in to him last night (my second call). The
first visit was one morning last week . . . He is very tall and stately,
with a fine firm chisel'd (how's that?) head, ordinary short brown
hair. The general expression of his face is one of boredom . . . After
leaving him, I wrote something in Sassoon's style, which I may as
well send you, since you ask for the latest.

The Dead-Beat (True—in the incidental)

> He dropped, more sullenly than wearily,
>   Became a lump of stench, a clot of meat,
>   And none of us could kick him to his feet.
> He blinked at my revolver, blearily.
>
> 5 He didn't seem to know a war was on,
>   Or see or smell the bloody trench at all . . .
>   Perhaps he saw the crowd at Caxton Hall,
>   And that is why the fellow's pluck's all gone—
>
> Not that the Kaiser frowns imperially.
> 10 He sees his wife, how cosily she chats;
>   Not his blue pal there, feeding fifty rats.
>   Hotels he sees, improved materially;
>
> Where ministers smile ministerially.
>   Sees Punch still grinning at the Belcher bloke;
> 15 Bairnsfather, enlarging on his little joke,
>   While Belloc prophecies of last year, serially.
>
> We sent him down at last, he seemed so bad,
>   Although a strongish chap and quite unhurt.
>   Next day I heard the Doc's fat laugh: 'That dirt
> 20 You sent me down last night's just died. So glad!'

These lines are years old!!

Those are the very words!

73

Next day

. . . He was struck with the 'Dead-Beat', but pointed out that the facetious bit was out of keeping with the first & last stanzas. Thus the piece as a whole is no good. Some of my old Sonnets didn't please him at all. But the 'Antæus' he applauded fervently; and a short lyric which I don't think you know 'Sing me at morn but only with thy Laugh' he pronounced perfect work, absolutely charming, etc. etc. and begged that I would copy it out for him, to show to the powers that be.

So the last thing he said was 'Sweat your guts out writing poetry!' 'Eh?' says I. 'Sweat your guts out, I say!'

Final draft:

The Dead-Beat

He dropped,—more sullenly than wearily,
Lay stupid like a cod, heavy like meat,
And none of us could kick him to his feet;
—Just blinked at my revolver, blearily;
5 —Didn't appear to know a war was on,
Or see the blasted trench at which he stared.
'I'll do 'em in,' he whined, 'if this hand's spared,
I'll murder them, I will.'

*　　*　　*

　　　　　　　　A low voice said,
'It's Blighty, p'raps, he sees; his pluck's all gone,
10 Dreaming of all the valiant, that *aren't* dead:
Bold uncles, smiling ministerially;
Maybe his brave young wife, getting her fun
In some new home, improved materially.
It's not these stiffs have crazed him; nor the Hun.'

*　　*　　*

15 We sent him down at last, out of the way.
Unwounded;—stout lad, too, before that strafe.
Malingering? Stretcher-bearers winked, 'Not half!'

*　　*　　*

Next day I heard the Doc.'s well-whiskied laugh:
'That scum you sent last night soon died. Hooray!'

The Letter

With B.E.F. June 10. Dear Wife,
(O blast this pencil. 'Ere, Bill, lend's a knife.)
I'm in the pink at present, dear.
I think the war will end this year.
5 We don't see much of them square-'eaded 'Uns.
We're out of harm's way, not bad fed.
I'm longing for a taste of your old buns.
(Say, Jimmie, spare's a bite of bread.)
There don't seem much to say just now.
10 (Yer what? Then don't, yer ruddy cow!
And give us back me cigarette!)
I'll soon be 'ome. You mustn't fret.
My feet's improvin', as I told you of.
We're out in rest now. Never fear.
15 (VRACH! By crumbs, but that was near.)
Mother might spare you half a sov.
Kiss Nell and Bert. When me and you—
(Eh? What the 'ell! Stand to? Stand to!
Jim, give's a hand with pack on, lad.
20 Guh! Christ! I'm hit. Take 'old. Aye, bad.
No, damn your iodine. Jim? 'Ere!
Write my old girl, Jim, there's a dear.)

The Next War

War's joke for me and you,
While we know such dreams are true.
SIEGFRIED SASSOON

Out there, we've walked quite friendly up to Death;
Sat down and eaten with him, cool and bland,—
Pardoned his spilling mess-tins in our hand.
We've sniffed the green thick odour of his breath,—
5 Our eyes wept, but our courage didn't writhe.
He's spat at us with bullets and he's coughed
Shrapnel. We chorussed when he sang aloft;
We whistled while he shaved us with his scythe.

75

Oh, Death was never enemy of ours!
10   We laughed at him, we leagued with him, old chum.
No soldier's paid to kick against his powers.
      We laughed, knowing that better men would come,
And greater wars; when each proud fighter brags
He wars on Death—for lives; not men—for flags.

Anthem for Doomed Youth

What passing-bells for these who die as cattle?
    —Only the monstrous anger of the guns.
    Only the stuttering rifles' rapid rattle
Can patter out their hasty orisons.
5 No mockeries now for them; no prayers nor bells;
    Nor any voice of mourning save the choirs,—
The shrill, demented choirs of wailing shells;
    And bugles calling for them from sad shires.

What candles may be held to speed them all?
10   Not in the hands of boys, but in their eyes
Shall shine the holy glimmers of good-byes.
    The pallor of girls' brows shall be their pall;
Their flowers the tenderness of patient minds,
And each slow dusk a drawing-down of blinds.

Disabled

He sat in a wheeled chair, waiting for dark,
And shivered in his ghastly suit of grey,
Legless, sewn short at elbow. Through the park
Voices of boys rang saddening like a hymn,
5 Voices of play and pleasure after day,
Till gathering sleep had mothered them from him. .

*   *   *

About this time Town used to swing so gay
When glow-lamps budded in the light blue trees,
And girls glanced lovelier as the air grew dim,—
10 In the old times, before he threw away his knees.
Now he will never feel again how slim
Girls' waists are, or how warm their subtle hands;
All of them touch him like some queer disease.

*   *   *

There was an artist silly for his face,
15 For it was younger than his youth, last year.
Now, he is old; his back will never brace;
He's lost his colour very far from here,
Poured it down shell-holes till the veins ran dry,
And half his lifetime lapsed in the hot race
20 And leap of purple spurted from his thigh.

*   *   *

One time he liked a blood-smear down his leg,
After the matches, carried shoulder-high.
It was after football, when he'd drunk a peg,
He thought he'd better join.—He wonders why.
25 Someone had said he'd look a god in kilts,
That's why; and may be, too, to please his Meg;
Aye, that was it, to please the giddy jilts
He asked to join. He didn't have to beg;
Smiling they wrote his lie; aged nineteen years.
30 Germans he scarcely thought of; all their guilt,
And Austria's, did not move him. And no fears
Of Fear came yet. He thought of jewelled hilts
For daggers in plaid socks; of smart salutes;
And care of arms; and leave; and pay arrears;
35 Esprit de corps; and hints for young recruits.
And soon, he was drafted out with drums and cheers.

*   *   *

Some cheered him home, but not as crowds cheer Goal.
Only a solemn man who brought him fruits
Thanked him; and then inquired about his soul.

*   *   *

40 Now, he will spend a few sick years in institutes,
And do what things the rules consider wise,
And take whatever pity they may dole.
To-night he noticed how the women's eyes
Passed from him to the strong men that were whole.
45 How cold and late it is! Why don't they come
And put him into bed? Why don't they come?

Conscious

His fingers wake, and flutter; up the bed.
His eyes come open with a pull of will,
Helped by the yellow may-flowers by his head.
The blind-cord drawls across the window-sill . . .
5 What a smooth floor the ward has! What a rug!
Who is that talking somewhere out of sight?
Why are they laughing? What's inside that jug?
'Nurse! Doctor!' — 'Yes; all right, all right.'

But sudden evening muddles all the air—
10 There seems no time to want a drink of water,
Nurse looks so far away. And here and there
Music and roses burst through crimson slaughter.
He can't remember where he saw blue sky.
More blankets. Cold. He's cold. And yet so hot.
15 And there's no light to see the voices by;
There is no time to ask—he knows not what.

Dulce Et Decorum Est

Bent double, like old beggars under sacks,
Knock-kneed, coughing like hags, we cursed through
                                 sludge,
Till on the haunting flares we turned our backs
And towards our distant rest began to trudge.
5 Men marched asleep. Many had lost their boots
But limped on, blood-shod. All went lame; all blind;
Drunk with fatigue; deaf even to the hoots
Of tired, outstripped Five-Nines that dropped behind.

Gas! GAS! Quick, boys!—An ecstasy of fumbling,
10 Fitting the clumsy helmets just in time;
But someone still was yelling out and stumbling,
And flound'ring like a man in fire or lime . . .
Dim, through the misty panes and thick green light,
As under a green sea, I saw him drowning.

15 In all my dreams, before my helpless sight,
He plunges at me, guttering, choking, drowning.

If in some smothering dreams you too could pace
Behind the wagon that we flung him in,
And watch the white eyes writhing in his face,
20 His hanging face, like a devil's sick of sin;
If you could hear, at every jolt, the blood
Come gargling from the froth-corrupted lungs,
Obscene as cancer, bitter as the cud
Of vile, incurable sores on innocent tongues,—
25 My friend, you would not tell with such high zest
To children ardent for some desperate glory,
The old Lie: Dulce et decorum est
Pro patria mori.

The Chances

I mind as 'ow the night afore that show
Us five got talkin',—we was in the know.
'Over the top to-morrer; boys, we're for it.
First wave we are, first ruddy wave; that's tore it!'
5 'Ah well,' says Jimmy,—an' 'e's seen some scrappin'—
'There ain't no more nor five things as can 'appen:
Ye get knocked out; else wounded—bad or cushy;
Scuppered; or nowt except yer feelin' mushy.'

*   *   *

One of us got the knock-out, blown to chops.
10 T'other was 'urt, like, losin' both 'is props.
An' one, to use the word of 'ypocrites,
'Ad the misfortoon to be took be Fritz.
Now me, I wasn't scratched, praise God Amighty,
(Though next time please I'll thank 'im for a blighty).
15 But poor young Jim, 'e's livin' an' 'e's not;
'E reckoned 'e'd five chances, an' 'e 'ad;
'E's wounded, killed, and pris'ner, all the lot,
The bloody lot all rolled in one. Jim's mad.

Soldier's Dream

I dreamed kind Jesus fouled the big-gun gears;
And caused a permanent stoppage in all bolts;
And buckled with a smile Mausers and Colts;
And rusted every bayonet with His tears.

5 And there were no more bombs, of ours or Theirs,
Not even an old flint-lock, nor even a pikel.
But God was vexed, and gave all power to Michael;
And when I woke he'd seen to our repairs.

Inspection

'You! What d'you mean by this?' I rapped.
'You dare come on parade like this?'
'Please, sir, it's——' ''Old yer mouth,' the sergeant
                                                    snapped.
'I takes 'is name, sir?'—'Please, and then dismiss.'

5 Some days 'confined to camp' he got,
For being 'dirty on parade'.
He told me, afterwards, the damnèd spot
Was blood, his own. 'Well, blood is dirt,' I said.

'Blood's dirt,' he laughed, looking away
10 Far off to where his wound had bled
And almost merged for ever into clay.
'The world is washing out its stains,' he said.
'It doesn't like our cheeks so red:
Young blood's its great objection.
15 But when we're duly white-washed, being dead,
The race will bear Field-Marshal God's inspection.'

Asleep

Under his helmet, up against his pack,
After the many days of work and waking,
Sleep took him by the brow and laid him back.
And in the happy no-time of his sleeping,
5 Death took him by the heart. There was a quaking
Of the aborted life within him leaping . . .
Then chest and sleepy arms once more fell slack.
And soon the slow, stray blood came creeping
From the intrusive lead, like ants on track.

*   *   *

10 Whether his deeper sleep lie shaded by the shaking
      Of great wings, and the thoughts that hung the stars,
      High pillowed on calm pillows of God's making
      Above these clouds, these rains, these sleets of lead,
      And these winds' scimitars;
15 —Or whether yet his thin and sodden head
      Confuses more and more with the low mould,
      His hair being one with the grey grass
      And finished fields of autumns that are old . . .
      Who knows? Who hopes? Who troubles? Let it pass!
20 He sleeps. He sleeps less tremulous, less cold
      Than we who must awake, and waking, say Alas!

Apologia pro Poemate Meo

I, too, saw God through mud,—
    The mud that cracked on cheeks when wretches smiled.
    War brought more glory to their eyes than blood,
    And gave their laughs more glee than shakes a child.

5 Merry it was to laugh there—
    Where death becomes absurd and life absurder.
    For power was on us as we slashed bones bare
    Not to feel sickness or remorse of murder.

    I, too, have dropped off Fear—
10   Behind the barrage, dead as my platoon,
    And sailed my spirit surging light and clear
    Past the entanglement where hopes lay strewn;

    And witnessed exultation—
    Faces that used to curse me, scowl for scowl,
15   Shine and lift up with passion of oblation,
    Seraphic for an hour; though they were foul.

    I have made fellowships—
    Untold of happy lovers in old song.
    For love is not the binding of fair lips
20   With the soft silk of eyes that look and long,

82

By Joy, whose ribbon slips, —
　　But wound with war's hard wire whose stakes are strong;
　　Bound with the bandage of the arm that drips;
　　Knit in the webbing of the rifle-thong.

25　I have perceived much beauty
　　In the hoarse oaths that kept our courage straight;
　　Heard music in the silentness of duty;
　　Found peace where shell-storms spouted reddest spate.

　　Nevertheless, except you share
30　With them in hell the sorrowful dark of hell,
　　Whose world is but the trembling of a flare
　　And heaven but as the highway for a shell,

　　You shall not hear their mirth:
　　You shall not come to think them well content
35　By any jest of mine. These men are worth
　　Your tears. You are not worth their merriment.

Hospital Barge at Cérisy

Budging the sluggard ripples of the Somme,
A barge round old Cérisy slowly slewed.
Softly her engines down the current screwed
And chuckled in her, with contented hum.

5　Till fairy tinklings struck their croonings dumb.
The waters rumpling at the stern subdued.
The lock-gate took her bulging amplitude.
Gently from out the gurgling lock she swum.

One reading by that sunset raised his eyes
10　To watch her lessening westward, quietly,
Till, as she neared the bend, her funnel screamed.

And that long lamentation made him wise
How unto Avalon, in agony,
Kings passed, in the dark barge, which Merlin dreamed.

Beauty

[Notes for an unfinished poem]

A shrapnel ball
Just where the wet skin glistened when he swam.
Like a full-opened sea-anemone.
We both said 'What a beauty! What a beauty, lad!'
5 I knew that in that flower he saw a hope
Of living on, and seeing again the roses of his home.
Beauty is that which pleases and delights
'Not bringing personal advantage'—Kant.
I laughed. But later on I heard
10 That a canker worked into that crimson flower
And that he sank with it [   ] over
And laid it with the anemones off Dover

[I saw his round mouth's crimson]

I saw his round mouth's crimson deepen as it fell,
    Like a Sun, in his last deep hour;
Watched the magnificent recession of farewell,
    Clouding, half gleam, half glower,
5 And a last splendour burn the heavens of his cheek.
    And in his eyes
The cold stars lighting, very old and bleak,
    In different skies.

[As bronze may be much beautified: a fragment]

As bronze may be much beautified
By lying in the dark damp soil,
So men who fade in dust of warfare fade
Fairer, and sorrow blooms their soul.

5 Like pearls which noble women wear
And, tarnishing, awhile confide
Unto the old salt sea to feed,
Many return more lustrous than they were.

But what of them buried profound,
10 Buried where we can no more find,
Who [   ]
Lie dark for ever under abysmal war?

[Cramped in that funnelled hole: a fragment]

Cramped in that funnelled hole, they watched the dawn
Open a jagged rim around; a yawn
Of death's jaws, which had all but swallowed them
Stuck in the bottom of his throat of phlegm.

5 They were in one of many mouths of Hell
Not seen of seers in visions; only felt
As teeth of traps; when bones and the dead are smelt
Under the mud where long ago they fell
Mixed with the sour sharp odour of the shell.

578. To Susan Owen

I am not dissatisfied with my years. Everything has been done in bouts:

Bouts of awful labour at Shrewsbury & Bordeaux; bouts of amazing pleasure in the Pyrenees, and play at Craiglockhart; bouts of religion at Dunsden; bouts of horrible danger on the Somme; bouts of poetry always; of your affection always; of sympathy for the oppressed always.

I go out of this year a Poet, my dear Mother, as which I did not enter it. I am held peer by the Georgians; I am a poet's poet.

I am started. The tugs have left me; I feel the great swelling of the open sea taking my galleon.

Last year, at this time, (it is just midnight, and now is the intolerable instant of the Change) last year I lay awake in a windy tent in the middle of a vast, dreadful encampment. It seemed neither France nor England, but a kind of paddock where the beasts are kept a few days before the shambles. I heard the revelling of the Scotch troops, who are now dead, and who knew they would be dead. I thought of this present night, and whether I should indeed—whether we should indeed—whether you would indeed—but I thought neither long nor deeply, for I am a master of elision.

But chiefly I thought of the very strange look on all faces in that camp; an incomprehensible look, which a man will never see in England, though wars should be in England; nor can it be seen in any battle. But only in Étaples.

It was not despair, or terror, it was more terrible than terror, for it was a blindfold look, and without expression, like a dead rabbit's.

It will never be painted, and no actor will ever seize it. And to describe it, I think I must go back and be with them.

583. To Susan Owen

With your beautiful letter came a proof from the *Nation* of my 'Miners'. This is the first poem I have sent to the *Nation* myself, and it has evidently been accepted. It was scrawled out on the back of a note to the Editor; and no penny stamp or addressed envelope was enclosed for return! That's the way to do it.

Miners

There was a whispering in my hearth,
    A sigh of the coal,
Grown wistful of a former earth
    It might recall.

5 I listened for a tale of leaves
    And smothered ferns;
Frond-forests; and the low, sly lives
    Before the fawns.

My fire might show steam-phantoms simmer
10   From Time's old cauldron,
Before the birds made nests in summer,
    Or men had children.

But the coals were murmuring of their mine,
    And moans down there
15 Of boys that slept wry sleep, and men
    Writhing for air.

And I saw white bones in the cinder-shard,
    Bones without number;
For many hearts with coal are charred;
20   And few remember.

I thought of some who worked dark pits
    Of war, and died
Digging the rock where Death reputes
    Peace lies indeed.

25 Comforted years will sit soft-chaired
    In rooms of amber:
The years will stretch their hands, well-cheered
    By our lives' ember.

The centuries will burn rich loads
30   With which we groaned,
Whose warmth shall lull their dreaming lids
    While songs are crooned.
But they will not dream of us poor lads,
    Lost in the ground.

The Last Laugh

'O Jesus Christ! I'm hit,' he said; and died.
Whether he vainly cursed, or prayed indeed,
The Bullets chirped—In vain! vain! vain!
Machine-guns chuckled,—Tut-tut! Tut-tut!
5 And the Big Gun guffawed.

Another sighed,—'O Mother, mother! Dad!'
Then smiled, at nothing, childlike, being dead.
    And the lofty Shrapnel-cloud
    Leisurely gestures,—Fool!
10   And the falling splinters tittered.

'My Love!' one moaned. Love-languid seemed his mood,
Till, slowly lowered, his whole face kissed the mud.
    And the Bayonets' long teeth grinned;
    Rabbles of Shells hooted and groaned;
15   And the Gas hissed.

First draft:

Last Words

'O Jesus Christ!' one fellow sighed.
And kneeled, and bowed, tho' not in prayer, and died.
    And the Bullets sang 'In Vain',
    Machine Guns chuckled 'Vain',
5   Big Guns guffawed 'In Vain'.

'Father and mother!' one boy said.
Then smiled—at nothing, like a small child; being dead.
    And the Shrapnel Cloud
    Slowly gestured 'Vain',
10   The falling splinters muttered 'Vain'.

'My love!' another cried, 'My love, my bud!'
Then, gently lowered, his whole face kissed the mud.
    And the Flares gesticulated, 'Vain',
    The Shells hooted, 'In Vain',
15   And the Gas hissed, 'In Vain'.

Insensibility

I

Happy are men who yet before they are killed
Can let their veins run cold.
Whom no compassion fleers
Or makes their feet
5 Sore on the alleys cobbled with their brothers.
The front line withers.
But they are troops who fade, not flowers,
For poets' tearful fooling:
Men, gaps for filling:
10 Losses, who might have fought
Longer; but no one bothers.

II

And some cease feeling
Even themselves or for themselves.
Dullness best solves
15 The tease and doubt of shelling,
And Chance's strange arithmetic
Comes simpler than the reckoning of their shilling.
They keep no check on armies' decimation.

III

Happy are these who lose imagination:
20 They have enough to carry with ammunition.
Their spirit drags no pack.
Their old wounds, save with cold, can not more ache.
Having seen all things red,
Their eyes are rid
25 Of the hurt of the colour of blood for ever.
And terror's first constriction over,
Their hearts remain small-drawn.
Their senses in some scorching cautery of battle
Now long since ironed,
30 Can laugh among the dying, unconcerned.

IV

Happy the soldier home, with not a notion
How somewhere, every dawn, some men attack,
And many sighs are drained.
Happy the lad whose mind was never trained:
35 His days are worth forgetting more than not.
He sings along the march
Which we march taciturn, because of dusk,
The long, forlorn, relentless trend
From larger day to huger night.

V

40 We wise, who with a thought besmirch
Blood over all our soul,
How should we see our task
But through his blunt and lashless eyes?
Alive, he is not vital overmuch;
45 Dying, not mortal overmuch;
Nor sad, nor proud,
Nor curious at all.
He cannot tell
Old men's placidity from his.

VI

50 But cursed are dullards whom no cannon stuns,
That they should be as stones.
Wretched are they, and mean
With paucity that never was simplicity.
By choice they made themselves immune
55 To pity and whatever mourns in man
Before the last sea and the hapless stars;
Whatever mourns when many leave these shores;
Whatever shares
The eternal reciprocity of tears.

Exposure

Our brains ache, in the merciless iced east winds that knive
    us . . .
Wearied we keep awake because the night is silent . . .
Low, drooping flares confuse our memory of the salient . . .
Worried by silence, sentries whisper, curious, nervous,
5   But nothing happens.

Watching, we hear the mad gusts tugging on the wire,
Like twitching agonies of men among its brambles.
Northward, incessantly, the flickering gunnery rumbles,
Far off, like a dull rumour of some other war.
10   What are we doing here?

The poignant misery of dawn begins to grow . . .
We only know war lasts, rain soaks, and clouds sag stormy.
Dawn massing in the east her melancholy army
Attacks once more in ranks on shivering ranks of gray,
15   But nothing happens.

Sudden successive flights of bullets streak the silence.
Less deathly than the air that shudders black with snow,
With sidelong flowing flakes that flock, pause, and renew;
We watch them wandering up and down the wind's non-
    chalance,
20   But nothing happens.

Pale flakes with fingering stealth come feeling for our
    faces—
We cringe in holes, back on forgotten dreams, and stare,
    snow-dazed,
Deep into grassier ditches. So we drowse, sun-dozed,
Littered with blossoms trickling where the blackbird fusses,
25   —Is it that we are dying?

Slowly our ghosts drag home: glimpsing the sunk fires,
    glozed
With crusted dark-red jewels; crickets jingle there;
For hours the innocent mice rejoice: the house is theirs;
Shutters and doors, all closed: on us the doors are closed,—
30   We turn back to our dying.

Since we believe not otherwise can kind fires burn;
Nor ever suns smile true on child, or field, or fruit.
For God's invincible spring our love is made afraid;
Therefore, not loath, we lie out here; therefore were born,
35   For love of God seems dying.

To-night, this frost will fasten on this mud and us,
Shrivelling many hands, puckering foreheads crisp.
The burying-party, picks and shovels in shaking grasp,
Pause over half-known faces. All their eyes are ice,
40   But nothing happens.

The Show

We have fallen in the dreams the ever-living
Breathe on the tarnished mirror of the world,
And then smooth out with ivory hands and sigh.
W. B. YEATS

My soul looked down from a vague height, with Death,
As unremembering how I rose or why,
And saw a sad land, weak with sweats of dearth,
Gray, cratered like the moon with hollow woe,
5 And pitted with great pocks and scabs of plagues.

Across its beard, that horror of harsh wire,
There moved thin caterpillars, slowly uncoiled.
It seemed they pushed themselves to be as plugs
Of ditches, where they writhed and shrivelled, killed.

10 By them had slimy paths been trailed and scraped
Round myriad warts that might be little hills.

From gloom's last dregs these long-strung creatures crept,
And vanished out of dawn down hidden holes.

(And smell came up from those foul openings
15 As out of mouths, or deep wounds deepening.)

92

On dithering feet upgathered, more and more,
Brown strings, towards strings of gray, with bristling spines,
All migrants from green fields, intent on mire.

Those that were gray, of more abundant spawns,
20 Ramped on the rest and ate them and were eaten.

I saw their bitten backs curve, loop, and straighten.
I watched those agonies curl, lift, and flatten.

Whereat, in terror what that sight might mean,
I reeled and shivered earthward like a feather.

25 And Death fell with me, like a deepening moan.

And He, picking a manner of worm, which half had hid
Its bruises in the earth, but crawled no further,
Showed me its feet, the feet of many men,
And the fresh-severed head of it, my head.

S.I.W.

> I will to the King,
> And offer him consolation in his trouble,
> For that man there has set his teeth to die,
> And being one that hates obedience,
> Discipline, and orderliness of life,
> I cannot mourn him.
> W. B. Yeats

I. THE PROLOGUE

Patting good-bye, doubtless they told the lad
He'd always show the Hun a brave man's face;
Father would sooner him dead than in disgrace,—
Was proud to see him going, aye, and glad.
5 Perhaps his mother whimpered how she'd fret
Until he got a nice safe wound to nurse.
Sisters would wish girls too could shoot, charge, curse . . .
Brothers—would send his favourite cigarette.
Each week, month after month, they wrote the same,

93

10 Thinking him sheltered in some Y.M. Hut,
   Because he said so, writing on his butt
   Where once an hour a bullet missed its aim
   And misses teased the hunger of his brain.
   His eyes grew old with wincing, and his hand
15 Reckless with ague. Courage leaked, as sand
   From the best sand-bags after years of rain.
   But never leave, wound, fever, trench-foot, shock,
   Untrapped the wretch. And death seemed still withheld
   For torture of lying machinally shelled,
20 At the pleasure of this world's Powers who'd run amok.

   He'd seen men shoot their hands, on night patrol.
   Their people never knew. Yet they were vile.
   'Death sooner than dishonour, that's the style!'
   So Father said.

II. THE ACTION
           One dawn, our wire patrol
25 Carried him. This time, Death had not missed.
   We could do nothing but wipe his bleeding cough.
   Could it be accident?—Rifles go off . . .
   Not sniped? No. (Later they found the English ball.)

III. THE POEM
   It was the reasoned crisis of his soul
30 Against more days of inescapable thrall,
   Against infrangibly wired and blind trench wall
   Curtained with fire, roofed in with creeping fire,
   Slow grazing fire, that would not burn him whole
   But kept him for death's promises and scoff,
35 And life's half-promising, and both their riling.

IV. THE EPILOGUE
   With him they buried the muzzle his teeth had kissed,
   And truthfully wrote the Mother, 'Tim died smiling'.

94

A Terre

(BEING THE PHILOSOPHY OF MANY SOLDIERS)

Sit on the bed. I'm blind, and three parts shell.
Be careful; can't shake hands now; never shall.
Both arms have mutinied against me,—brutes.
My fingers fidget like ten idle brats.

5 I tried to peg out soldierly,—no use!
One dies of war like any old disease.
This bandage feels like pennies on my eyes.
I have my medals?—Discs to make eyes close.
My glorious ribbons?—Ripped from my own back
10 In scarlet shreds. (That's for your poetry book.)

A short life and a merry one, my buck!
We used to say we'd hate to live dead-old,—
Yet now . . . I'd willingly be puffy, bald,
And patriotic. Buffers catch from boys
15 At least the jokes hurled at them. I suppose
Little I'd ever teach a son, but hitting,
Shooting, war, hunting, all the arts of hurting.
Well, that's what I learnt,—that, and making money.

Your fifty years ahead seem none too many?
20 Tell me how long I've got? God! For one year
To help myself to nothing more than air!
One Spring! Is one too good to spare, too long?
Spring wind would work its own way to my lung,
And grow me legs as quick as lilac-shoots.

25 My servant's lamed, but listen how he shouts!
When I'm lugged out, he'll still be good for that.
Here in this mummy-case, you know, I've thought
How well I might have swept his floors for ever.
I'd ask no nights off when the bustle's over,
30 Enjoying so the dirt. Who's prejudiced
Against a grimed hand when his own's quite dust,
Less live than specks that in the sun-shafts turn,

Less warm than dust that mixes with arms' tan?
I'd love to be a sweep, now, black as Town,
35 Yes, or a muckman. Must I be his load?

O Life, Life, let me breathe,—a dug-out rat!
Not worse than ours the existences rats lead—
Nosing along at night down some safe rut,
They find a shell-proof home before they rot.
40 Dead men may envy living mites in cheese,
Or good germs even. Microbes have their joys,
And subdivide, and never come to death.
Certainly flowers have the easiest time on earth.
'I shall be one with nature, herb, and stone,'
45 Shelley would tell me. Shelley would be stunned:
The dullest Tommy hugs that fancy now.
'Pushing up daisies' is their creed, you know.

To grain, then, go my fat, to buds my sap,
For all the usefulness there is in soap.
50 D'you think the Boche will ever stew man-soup?
Some day, no doubt, if . . .

                                        Friend, be very sure
I shall be better off with plants that share
More peaceably the meadow and the shower.
Soft rains will touch me,—as they could touch once,
55 And nothing but the sun shall make me ware.
Your guns may crash around me. I'll not hear;
Or, if I wince, I shall not know I wince.

Don't take my soul's poor comfort for your jest.
Soldiers may grow a soul when turned to fronds,
60 But here the thing's best left at home with friends.

My soul's a little grief, grappling your chest,
To climb your throat on sobs; easily chased
On other sighs and wiped by fresher winds.

Carry my crying spirit till it's weaned
65 To do without what blood remained these wounds.

Arms and the Boy

Let the boy try along this bayonet-blade
How cold steel is, and keen with hunger of blood;
Blue with all malice, like a madman's flash;
And thinly drawn with famishing for flesh.

5 Lend him to stroke these blind, blunt bullet-leads
Which long to nuzzle in the hearts of lads,
Or give him cartridges of fine zinc teeth,
Sharp with the sharpness of grief and death.

For his teeth seem for laughing round an apple.
10 There lurk no claws behind his fingers supple;
And God will grow no talons at his heels,
Nor antlers through the thickness of his curls.

The Send-Off

Down the close darkening lanes they sang their way
To the siding-shed,
And lined the train with faces grimly gay.

Their breasts were stuck all white with wreath and spray
5 As men's are, dead.

Dull porters watched them, and a casual tramp
Stood staring hard,
Sorry to miss them from the upland camp.

Then, unmoved, signals nodded, and a lamp
10 Winked to the guard.

So secretly, like wrongs hushed-up, they went.
They were not ours:
We never heard to which front these were sent.

Nor there if they yet mock what women meant
15 Who gave them flowers.

Shall they return to beatings of great bells
In wild train-loads?
A few, a few, too few for drums and yells,

May creep back, silent, to still village wells
20 Up half-known roads.

Futility

Move him into the sun—
Gently its touch awoke him once,
At home, whispering of fields unsown.
Always it woke him, even in France,
5 Until this morning and this snow.
If anything might rouse him now
The kind old sun will know.

Think how it wakes the seeds,—
Woke, once, the clays of a cold star.
10 Are limbs, so dear-achieved, are sides,
Full-nerved,—still warm,—too hard to stir?
Was it for this the clay grew tall?
—O what made fatuous sunbeams toil
To break earth's sleep at all?

Mental Cases

Who are these? Why sit they here in twilight?
Wherefore rock they, purgatorial shadows,
Drooping tongues from jaws that slob their relish,
Baring teeth that leer like skulls' teeth wicked?
5 Stroke on stroke of pain,—but what slow panic,
Gouged these chasms round their fretted sockets?
Ever from their hair and through their hands' palms
Misery swelters. Surely we have perished
Sleeping, and walk hell; but who these hellish?

10 —These are men whose minds the Dead have ravished.
Memory fingers in their hair of murders,
Multitudinous murders they once witnessed.
Wading sloughs of flesh these helpless wander,
Treading blood from lungs that had loved laughter.
15 Always they must see these things and hear them,
Batter of guns and shatter of flying muscles,
Carnage incomparable, and human squander
Rucked too thick for these men's extrication.

Therefore still their eyeballs shrink tormented
20 Back into their brains, because on their sense
Sunlight seems a blood-smear; night comes blood-black;
Dawn breaks open like a wound that bleeds afresh.
—Thus their heads wear this hilarious, hideous,
Awful falseness of set-smiling corpses.
25 —Thus their hands are plucking at each other;
Picking at the rope-knouts of their scourging;
Snatching after us who smote them, brother,
Pawing us who dealt them war and madness.

The Kind Ghosts

She sleeps on soft, last breaths; but no ghost looms
Out of the stillness of her palace wall,
Her wall of boys on boys and dooms on dooms.

She dreams of golden gardens and sweet glooms,
5 Not marvelling why her roses never fall
Nor what red mouths were torn to make their blooms.

The shades keep down which well might roam her hall.
Quiet their blood lies in her crimson rooms
And she is not afraid of their footfall.

10 They move not from her tapestries, their pall,
Nor pace her terraces, their hecatombs,
Lest aught she be disturbed, or grieved at all.

The Calls

A dismal fog-hoarse siren howls at dawn.
I watch the man it calls for, pushed and drawn
Backwards and forwards, helpless as a pawn.
    But I'm lazy, and his work's crazy.

5 Quick treble bells begin at nine o'clock,
Scuttling the schoolboy pulling up his sock,
Scaring the late girl in the inky frock.
    I must be crazy; I learn from the daisy.

Stern bells annoy the rooks and doves at ten.
10 I watch the verger close the doors, and when
I hear the organ moan the first amen,
    Sing my religion's—same as pigeons'.

A blatant bugle tears my afternoons.
Out clump the clumsy Tommies by platoons,
15 Trying to keep in step with rag-time tunes,
    But I sit still; I've done my drill.

Gongs hum and buzz like saucepan-lids at dusk.
I see a food-hog whet his gold-filled tusk
To eat less bread, and more luxurious rusk.
20   [   ]

Then sometimes late at night my window bumps
From gunnery-practice, till my small heart thumps
And listens for the shell-shrieks and the crumps,
    But that's not all.

25 For leaning out last midnight on my sill,
I heard the sighs of men, that have no skill
To speak of their distress, no, nor the will!
    A voice I know. And this time I must go.

641. To Susan Owen

I send you a precious letter, from the Greatest friend I have.

I was inoculated again on Sat. but it was Siegfried's condition and not my own that made me so wretched. This time surely he has done with war.

The most encouraging thing is that he is writing already again.

Now must I throw my little candle on his torch, and go out again.

There are rumours of a large draft of officers shortly.

643. To Susan Owen

10 August 1918   *Scarborough*

Tomorrow I am for a medical inspection with 21 others, to be declared fit for draft. This means we may be sent on draft leave tomorrow, & I may reach you even before this letter! I know not. I am glad. That is I am much gladder to be going out again than afraid. I shall be better able to cry my outcry, playing my part.

. . . this morning at 8.20 we heard a boat torpedoed in the bay about a mile out, they say who saw it. I think only 10 lives were saved. I wish the Bosche would have the pluck to come right in & make a clean sweep of the Pleasure Boats, and the promenaders on the Spa, and all the stinking Leeds & Bradford War-profiteers now reading *John Bull* on Scarborough Sands.

647. To Susan Owen

31 August 1918   *E.F.C., Officers Rest House and Mess*

And now I go among cattle to be a cattle-driver . . .

I am now fairly and reasonably tired & must go to my tent, without saying the things which you will better understand unsaid.

> O my heart,
> Be still; You have cried your cry, you played your part.

Did I ever send you Siegfried's poem which he wrote on the boat:

> For the last time I say War is not glorious;
> Tho' lads march out superb & die victorious,

And crowned by peace, the sunlight on their graves;
    You say we crush the Beast; I say we fight
    Because men lost their landmarks in the night,
    And met in gloom to grapple, stab & kill.
    Yelling the fetish names of Good & Ill
    Which have been shamed in history.

        O my heart,
Be still; you have cried your cry, you have played your part!

Goodnight, goodnight.
You are at home; yet you are home;
Your love is my home, and $\overline{\text{I}}$ cannot feel abroad.

Strange Meeting

It seemed that out of battle I escaped
Down some profound dull tunnel, long since scooped
Through granites which titanic wars had groined.

Yet also there encumbered sleepers groaned,
5 Too fast in thought or death to be bestirred.
Then, as I probed them, one sprang up, and stared
With piteous recognition in fixed eyes,
Lifting distressful hands, as if to bless.
And by his smile, I knew that sullen hall, —
10 By his dead smile I knew we stood in Hell.

With a thousand pains that vision's face was grained;
Yet no blood reached there from the upper ground,
And no guns thumped, or down the flues made moan.
'Strange friend,' I said, 'here is no cause to mourn.'
15 'None,' said that other, 'save the undone years,
The hopelessness. Whatever hope is yours,
Was my life also; I went hunting wild
After the wildest beauty in the world,
Which lies not calm in eyes, or braided hair,
20 But mocks the steady running of the hour,

And if it grieves, grieves richlier than here.
For by my glee might many men have laughed,
And of my weeping something had been left,
Which must die now. I mean the truth untold,
25 The pity of war, the pity war distilled.
Now men will go content with what we spoiled,
Or, discontent, boil bloody, and be spilled.
They will be swift with swiftness of the tigress.
None will break ranks, though nations trek from progress.
30 Courage was mine, and I had mystery,
Wisdom was mine, and I had mastery:
To miss the march of this retreating world
Into vain citadels that are not walled.
Then, when much blood had clogged their chariot-wheels,
35 I would go up and wash them from sweet wells,
Even with truths that lie too deep for taint.
I would have poured my spirit without stint
But not through wounds; not on the cess of war.
Foreheads of men have bled where no wounds were.

40 I am the enemy you killed, my friend.
I knew you in this dark: for so you frowned
Yesterday through me as you jabbed and killed.
I parried; but my hands were loath and cold.
Let us sleep now. . . .'

The Sentry

We'd found an old Boche dug-out, and he knew,
And gave us hell, for shell on frantic shell
Hammered on top, but never quite burst through.
Rain, guttering down in waterfalls of slime,
5 Kept slush waist-high and rising hour by hour,
And choked the steps too thick with clay to climb.
What murk of air remained stank old, and sour
With fumes of whizz-bangs, and the smell of men
Who'd lived there years, and left their curse in the den,
10 If not their corpses . . .

     There we herded from the blast
Of whizz-bangs, but one found our door at last,
Buffeting eyes and breath, snuffing the candles,
And thud! flump! thud! down the steep steps came
                                        thumping
And sploshing in the flood, deluging muck—
15 The sentry's body; then, his rifle, handles
Of old Boche bombs, and mud in ruck on ruck.
We dredged him up, for killed, until he whined
'O sir, my eyes—I'm blind,—I'm blind, I'm blind!'
Coaxing, I held a flame against his lids
20 And said if he could see the least blurred light
He was not blind; in time he'd get all right.
'I can't,' he sobbed. Eyeballs, huge-bulged like squids',
Watch my dreams still; but I forgot him there
In posting Next for duty, and sending a scout
25 To beg a stretcher somewhere, and flound'ring about
To other posts under the shrieking air.

                *   *   *

Those other wretches, how they bled and spewed,
And one who would have drowned himself for good,—
I try not to remember these things now.
30 Let dread hark back for one word only: how
Half-listening to that sentry's moans and jumps,
And the wild chattering of his broken teeth,
Renewed most horribly whenever crumps
Pummelled the roof and slogged the air beneath,—
35 Through the dense din, I say, we heard him shout
'I see your lights!' But ours had long died out.

666. To Susan Owen

11 October 1918   *2nd Manchester Regt.*

That time on the Somme in 1917 was so infinitely worse than this
for cold, privation and fatigue that nothing daunts me now.

The Sergeant, now acting my Coy. Sgt. Major, was a corporal
with me in the first dug-out where the Sentry was blinded, you
remember. He remembers it . . .

660. To Siegfried Sassoon

22 September 1918   *D Coy. 2nd Manchester Regt.*

My dear Siegfried,

Here are a few poems to tempt you to a letter. I begin to think your correspondence must be intercepted somewhere. So I will state merely

I have had no letter from you $\begin{cases} \text{lately} \\ \text{for a long time,} \end{cases}$

and say nothing of my situation, tactical or personal.

You said it would be a good thing for my poetry if I went back.

That is my consolation for feeling a fool. This is what the shells scream at me every time: Haven't you got the wits to keep out of this?

Did you see what the Minister of Labour said in the *Mail* the other day?

'The first instincts of the men after the cessation of hostilities will be to return home.' And again—

'All classes acknowledge their indebtedness to the soldiers & sailors . . .'

About the same day, Clemenceau [Prime Minister of France] is reported by the *Times* as saying: 'All are worthy . . . yet we should be untrue to ourselves if we forgot that the greatest glory will be to the splendid poilus, who, etc.'

I began a postscript to these Confessions, but hope you will already have lashed yourself, (lashed yourself!) into something . . .

O Siegfried, make them Stop!*

W. E. O.

P.S. My Mother's address is Mahim
Monkmoor Rd. Shrewsbury.

I know you would try to see her, if—— I failed to see her again.

---

* Cf. 'O Jesus, make it stop!' (Sassoon, *Attack*).

672. To Susan Owen

29 October 1918   *2nd Manchester Regt.*

Did I tell you that five healthy girls died of fright in one night at
the last village. The people in England and France who thwarted a
peaceable retirement of the enemy from these areas are therefore
now sacrificing aged French peasants and charming French children
to our guns. Shells made by women in Birmingham are at this
moment burying little children alive not very far from here.

Smile, smile, smile

Head to limp head, the sunk-eyed wounded scanned
Yesterday's *Mail*; the casualties (typed small)
And (large) Vast Booty from our latest Haul.
Also, they read of Cheap Homes, not yet planned,
5 'For,' said the paper, 'when this war is done
The men's first instinct will be making homes.
Meanwhile their foremost need is aerodromes,
It being certain war has but begun.
Peace would do wrong to our undying dead, —
10 The sons we offered might regret they died
If we got nothing lasting in their stead.
We must be solidly indemnified.
Though all be worthy Victory which all bought,
We rulers sitting in this ancient spot
15 Would wrong our very selves if we forgot
The greatest glory will be theirs who fought,
Who kept this nation in integrity.'
Nation? — The half-limbed readers did not chafe
But smiled at one another curiously
20 Like secret men who know their secret safe.
(This is the thing they know and never speak,
That England one by one had fled to France,
Not many elsewhere now, save under France.)
Pictures of these broad smiles appear each week,
25 And people in whose voice real feeling rings
Say: How they smile! They're happy now, poor things.

662. To Susan Owen

Strictly private

My darling Mother,

As you must have known both by my silence and from the news-papers which mention this Division—and perhaps by other means & senses—I have been in action for some days.

I can find no word to qualify my experiences except the word SHEER. (Curiously enough I find the papers* talk about sheer fighting!) It passed the limits of my Abhorrence. I lost all my earthly faculties, and fought like an angel.

If I started into detail of our engagement I should disturb the censor and my own Rest.

You will guess what has happened when I say I am now Command-ing the Company, and in the line had a boy lance-corporal as my Sergeant-Major.

With this corporal who stuck to me and shadowed me like your prayers I captured a German Machine Gun and scores of prisoners.

I'll tell you exactly how another time. I only shot one man with my revolver (at about 30 yards!); The rest I took with a smile. The same thing happened with other parties all along the line we entered.

I have been recommended for the Military Cross; and have recommended every single N.C.O. who was with me!

My nerves are in perfect order.

I came out in order to help these boys—directly by leading them as well as an officer can; indirectly, by watching their sufferings that I may speak of them as well as a pleader can. I have done the first.

Of whose blood lies yet crimson on my shoulder where his head was—and where so lately yours was—I must not now write.

It is all over for a long time. We are marching steadily back.
Moreover
The War is nearing an end.
Still,

Wilfred and more than Wilfred

---

* ADVANCE BY SHEER FIGHTING. *Daily Mail* headline, 19 September 1918.

Spring Offensive

Halted against the shade of a last hill,
They fed, and lying easy, were at ease
And, finding comfortable chests and knees,
Carelessly slept. But many there stood still
5 To face the stark blank sky beyond the ridge,
Knowing their feet had come to the end of the world.

Marvelling they stood, and watched the long grass swirled
By the May breeze, murmurous with wasp and midge,
For though the summer oozed into their veins
10 Like an injected drug for their bodies' pains,
Sharp on their souls hung the imminent line of grass,
Fearfully flashed the sky's mysterious glass.

Hour after hour they ponder the warm field,—
And the far valley behind, where the buttercup
15 Had blessed with gold their slow boots coming up,
Where even the little brambles would not yield
But clutched and clung to them like sorrowing hands.
[   ] they breathe like trees unstirred.

Till like a cold gust thrills the little word
20 At which each body and its soul begird
And tighten them for battle. No alarms
Of bugles, no high flags, no clamorous haste,—
Only a lift and flare of eyes that faced
The sun, like a friend with whom their love is done.
25 O larger shone that smile against the sun,—
Mightier than his whose bounty these have spurned.

So, soon they topped the hill, and raced together
Over an open stretch of herb and heather
Exposed. And instantly the whole sky burned
30 With fury against them; earth set sudden cups
In thousands for their blood; and the green slope
Chasmed and steepened sheer to infinite space.

Of them who running on that last high place
Leapt to swift unseen bullets, or went up
35 On the hot blast and fury of hell's upsurge,
Or plunged and fell away past this world's verge,
Some say God caught them even before they fell.

But what say such as from existence' brink
Ventured but drave too swift to sink,
40 The few who rushed in the body to enter hell,
And there out-fiending all its fiends and flames
With superhuman inhumanities,
Long-famous glories, immemorial shames—
And crawling slowly back, have by degrees
45 Regained cool peaceful air in wonder—
Why speak not they of comrades that went under?

NOTES ON THE POEMS

ABBREVIATIONS:

WO: Wilfred Owen.

SS: Siegfried Sassoon.

EB: Edmund Blunden, or his edition of the poems, 1931.

CDL: C. Day Lewis, or his edition of the poems, 1963.

DSRW: D. S. R. Welland, in *Wilfred Owen: a Critical Study*.

Letters: Wilfred Owen: Collected Letters, ed. Harold Owen and John Bell.

BM: The collection of Owen's manuscripts in the British Museum.

On My Songs. p. 51. A poem interesting in its biographical context. It marks WO's first major nervous crisis, the break at Dunsden from evangelical religion and his mother's influence; the image of the motherless child in the sestet is a very personal one. Already conscious of writing and behaving like some of the Romantic poets, WO is nevertheless finding the need for a style and voice of his own. Underneath the derivative and conventional style of the sonnet, strong feeling is struggling to make itself heard. See *Letters*, p. 160, for a sonnet on Keats by J. R. Lowell which WO seems to have in mind here. This is the CDL text, with minor emendations.

l. 13. *the Dark*: an early use of the theme of darkness that plays so large a part in the later poems.

O World of many worlds. p. 52. A draft of the last three stanzas is printed as a separate poem entitled *This is the Track* by EB and CDL. It is possible that these stanzas were composed before the rest; they incorporate part of a verse from the Bible (*wandering stars, to whom is reserved the blackness of darkness for ever.* Jude, 13). WO quotes from this verse in Letter 185, April 1913; the poem may well have been written in that year. See Introduction, p. 31. A number of small errors in the CDL text have been corrected. Title: Titles enclosed in square brackets are additions by various editors to poems left untitled by WO.

l. 11. *floor*: cf. the floor in the temple of Saturn (Keats, *The Fall of Hyperion*).

l. 13. cf. *The Show*.

ll. 21-24. cf. *Strange Meeting*, ll. 29 and 32.

ll. 27-28. cf. *Storm*, l. 12; and WO's Preface (*All a poet can do today is warn*).

l. 40. cf. *Spring Offensive*, l. 26.

Storm. p. 54. A powerful but obscure sonnet. Who is the *he* referred to? A lover; a fellow-poet; Apollo, god of poetry and beauty (cf. Keats's *Hyperion*); war? The poet sees himself as a tree drawing lightning, which is the beauty in someone's face; this beauty is godlike but destructive—after an instant's brilliance, the tree will fall. The instant, however, brings truth as well as beauty (*the opening of my heart* describes both the splitting open of the tree and the self-revelation of the poet in his moment of glory). MS dated *Oct. 1916*.

l. 12. Cf.   *Men started, staggering with a glad surprise,*
             Under the lightnings of thine unfamiliar eyes.

(Shelley, *Ode to Liberty*, XI)

l. 14. *hilarious*: WO's poems are full of strange references to laughter. Cf. l. 6 and *Strange Meeting*, l. 22.

Music. p. 54. Drafted at least six times. The final draft is dated *Oct. 1916-17* and was perhaps one of the collection of sonnets reworked at Craiglockhart for SS's approval. 'Music' was one of the cousins' set subjects. Translating emotional experience into musical imagery appealed strongly to WO.

l. 6. *gods'*: other editions have *God's*. All five BM drafts show a small *g*; the placing of the apostrophe is ambiguous, however. Earlier drafts show that these lines describe playing the organ.

ll. 6-8: *thunder—winds—pondered—maundered—wandered*: a sound-sequence very typical of WO's style during these years. In his later poems he uses a similar technique with far more subtlety.

Maundy Thursday. p. 55. CDL suggests this might be a Dunsden poem; but the Vicar was a strict evangelical and would surely not have permitted his flock to kiss a crucifix. WO attended Mass at Christmas and Easter at Mérignac and wrote home, in a tone of amused contempt, about Roman Catholic ritual; his only diversion was to watch the *acolytes* trying to keep awake. The sonnet may therefore be taken as a fairly light-hearted comment on Roman Catholic practices rather than as a serious criticism of religion in general.

Shadwell Stair. p. 55. No one has yet dated this poem or explained its origin. It bears a marked similarity to Oscar Wilde's *Impression du Matin* and may have been a deliberate imitation. Shadwell Dock Stair is one of the many flights of steps leading from quay to water's edge along that part of the Thames known as the Pool of London. The identity of the *ghost* has yet to be established.

l. 7. *full*: thus final draft. EB gives *lapping* and *dripping* for *cavernous* (l. 3).

From My Diary, July 1914. p. 56. WO arrived in the Pyrenees at the end of July 1914 and was delighted with his new surroundings. A few days later, war was declared. WO put the date in the title perhaps to remind his readers that he is describing the last days of peace. Critics have, rather rashly, assumed that the poem was actually written in July 1914 and have therefore accepted it as the earliest surviving example of WO's use of pararhyme. In addition to the pararhymes of the short lines, each of the long lines contains elaborate alliteration or assonance or both.

ll. 1-4. WO never finished these lines. The version given here is EB's reconstruction.

1914. p. 58. Apparently WO's first poem to do with the war. There are four drafts, one called *The Seed* and dated 1914. For later versions of the *wild Winter* and spring of war, cf. *Exposure* and *Spring Offensive*.

l. 1. Cf. *This is the winter of the world;—and here We die* (Shelley, *Revolt of Islam*, IX, 25). WO also uses the phrase in Letter 425.

l. 2. *perishing great darkness*: another image of darkness, this time applied to war rather than to poetic experience, almost as though WO sensed that war and poetic experience were to become the same thing for him.

l. 12. Cf. *The teeming autumn, big with rich increase* (Shakespeare, Sonnet 97).

The Unreturning. p. 58. The poem remains undated and the MS from which EB took this version seems to be lost.

l. 10. In an early letter (111), WO had referred to the belief that sick men are at their weakest and most likely to die at 3 a.m. Cf. *Insensibility*, ll. 32-33.

Sonnet. p. 61. The word *Heavy* is quite clear in the one BM draft, but both EB and CDL omit it from the title without explanation. The rhetorical language might suggest an early 1917 date; and in l. 5 WO makes one of his remarkably rare criticisms of Germany. The sestet, however, shows the beginning of his later attitude to war.

Happiness. p. 66. 'I am settling down to a little verse once more, and tonight I want to do Leslie's subject "Golden Hair" and O.A.J.'s "Happiness" ' (Letter 484, 12th February 1917). These two poems (*Golden Hair* is in BM) are the first WO wrote after experiencing fighting.

ll. 1-2. First draft has:

> *Ever to know unhoping happiness*
> *Harboured in heaven, being a Mother's boy.*

ll. 12-14. 'Not before January 1917 did I write the *only lines* of mine that carry the stamp of maturity' [and WO then quotes a version of these lines] (Letter 538, 8th August 1917). The maternal imagery of the poem (cf. *On My Songs*) shows WO's awareness that he has passed beyond his mother's help at last. *Happiness* seems to have been revised over a long period. EB gives the second version of the sestet, from a draft now in the Bodleian; CDL prefers the first (BM).

Sonnet to my Friend. p. 67. Each soldier was issued with three identity discs to be worn on a cord round the neck. If he was killed, one disc was sent to his next of kin; the sonnet is supposed to be sent with this disc. Drafted in March 1917 in an exercise book used for other poems at the C.C.S. In the same book WO wrote from memory Shakespeare's sonnet *To me, fair friend, you never can be old*; his own sonnet shows Shakespeare's influence. This is EB's conflation from two of several scrappy drafts.
l. 2. Two drafts suggest WO refers to an ambition to earn himself a memorial in Poets' Corner, Westminster Abbey.
ll. 7-8. Keats's grave in the Protestant Cemetery, Rome, lies among cypress trees.

The End. p. 67. 'Leslie tells me that Miss Joergens considers my Sonnet on *The End* the finest of the lot. Naturally, because it is, intentionally, in her style!' (Letter 484, February 1917). *The End* is certainly not in WO's most characteristic style (compare it with *The Unreturning*, for example), although it contains traces of Shelley (cf. the Earth in *Prometheus Unbound*, III, iii, 88-89: *through my withered, old, and icy frame/The warmth of an immortal* *youth shoots down*). Critics and anthologists have perhaps rated *The End* too highly; it appears, judging from MSS, to have been first written before 1917 and later much revised. Possibly it was not in origin a poem about the war, but WO saw that it could be read as a war poem and included it under 'Doubtful' in his Table of Contents.

ll. 5-6. WO's tombstone at Ors bears the inscription:

> *Shall life renew these bodies? Of a truth*
> *All death will He annul.*

Mrs Owen was responsible for the choice of quotation and, if understandably, for the highly misleading change in punctuation.

l. 10. This short line was originally of an orthodox length; WO wrote *everlasting* before *snow* but crossed it out.

Greater Love. p. 68. 'Greater love hath no man than this, that a man lay down his life for his friends' (*John* xv, 13). A cancelled title on one of the six drafts reads *To any beautiful Woman*. The love that the soldiers show in sacrificing themselves is greater than that shown by a lover and as great as that shown by Christ himself; in the second stanza, the soldiers' death is compared, some critics claim, to the sexual act and, in l. 10, to the supreme sacrifice of the Crucifixion (cf. 'My God, my God, why hast thou forsaken me?' *Matt.* xxvii, 46; and l. 23). Included only under 'Doubtful' in WO's Table of Contents, this poem probably should not be taken as one of his final interpretations of war—see Introduction, p. 37.

Perhaps more than any other poem by Owen, *Greater Love* has aroused widely differing critical responses. Some people admire it highly; some find it gruesome and sickly. It is certainly remarkably original in its elaborate parallels between sexual lover, soldier and Christ. The pale hand and soft voice of the traditional female lover in Romantic poetry, for example, become the bloodless hand and choking last words of the dying soldier; at the same time we are reminded of Christ's hand trailing his cross through the streets of Jerusalem and of his cry of despair during the agony of death.

ll. 1-2. Cf. *White rose in the red rose-garden/Is not so white* (Swinburne, *Behind the Mirror*).

The Parable of the Old Man and the Young. p. 69. For the original story of Abraham and Isaac, see *Genesis* xxii, 1-19; and for similar adaptations of Biblical themes, compare Graves' *Goliath and David* (in which the former kills the latter) and Osbert Sitwell's *The Modern Abraham*. No evidence as to date, except that WO sent the poem to Sitwell in summer 1918. The style lacks WO's usual originality, perhaps only because he is adhering very closely to the wording of the story in *Genesis*.

l. 14. *the Ram of Pride*: the older generation should sacrifice its nationalistic pride and not its young men, as Abraham slew the ram instead of Isaac.

Le Christianisme. p. 70. MS marked *Quivières*, where WO was quartered in April 1917 immediately after Fayet. These lines are thus likely to have been written during the initial stages of shell-shock. The *church Christ* makes an ironic contrast with the crossroads Christ in *At a Calvary*.

At a Calvary near the Ancre. p. 70. Calvary, or Golgotha, was the site of the Crucifixion; a calvary is a lifelike model of the Crucifixion often set up at crossroads in Roman Catholic countries. WO was involved in the fighting near the River Ancre in early 1917. The original MS of the poem is lost, so that one cannot date it.

As in *The Parable of the Old Man and the Young*, WO adapts Biblical detail to fit the war. In the Gospel story, the *Soldiers* kept watch at the cross while Christ's *disciples* hid in fear of the authorities; *priests* and *scribes* passed by in scorn. The Church sends priests to the trenches, where they watch the common soldier being, as it were, crucified, and they take pride in minor wounds (*flesh-marked*, l. 7) as a sign of their opposition to Germany (*the Beast*). *Flesh-marked*, however, carries a further meaning: the Devil used to be believed to leave his finger-marks on the flesh of his followers (cf. *Revelation* xiv, 9-10). Thus the Church's hatred of Germany (l. 12) puts it in the Devil's following; and the priests' wounds are signs not so much of opposition to the Devil Germany as of allegiance to the Devil War. Christ said 'Love one another' *and* 'Love your enemies'; despite the exhortations of Church and State, WO perceives that 'pure Christianity will not fit in with pure patriotism' (Letter 512, p. 68). For examples of the popular view of the soldier as Christ, cf. the wartime poems of 'John Oxenham'; WO came to regard such verse with contempt (Letter 521).

Six o'clock in Princes Street. p. 71. Surviving notes for the poem show that WO's original intention was to satirise the indifference to war of the civilian crowds strolling in the main street:

> *Princes St., Edinburgh*
> *The Sunday crowd, by families and couples,*
> *Enjoy the air. They are resigned to war*
> *For them the war is but a chalking of the pavement.*
> *Gas-driven busses*
> > *sugarless tea   enslavement*
> *But plenty of handsome men in kilts and trews*

The final poem abandons this rather facile approach and becomes a statement of WO's role as a poet and of his sympathy for the crowds and for the newsboy, who is developed from mere headlines chalked on the pavement into a symbol of human suffering with whom WO, another news-bearer, would identify himself if he 'dared' leave what he still considers to be his task as poet. For the imagery of the poem, see Introduction, p. 31; for its form and some of its language, cf. Yeats's *When you are old* which WO must have had in mind.

Antaeus: a fragment. p. 71. WO's doctor at Craiglockhart set him, as a therapeutic exercise, the task of writing a blank-verse poem on the subject of Antaeus, the giant and wrestler of classical myth. Antaeus was a son of Earth and could renew his strength by touching the ground; he was eventually defeated by Hercules, who held him up in the air and crushed him to death. WO sent this fragment home on 17th July 1917 and said that 50 lines were by then completed.

Song of Songs. p. 72. This exercise in pararhymed triplets was written at Craiglockhart; WO showed it to SS at their first meeting. SS singled it out for enthusiastic praise 'as a musical achievement not possible to him' (Letter 545) and WO promptly published it in *The Hydra*. It thus became the first of WO's poems to be printed; in May 1918 it was published again, in *The Bookman*, and won a consolation prize in a competition—but by then WO thought little of it (Letters 618, 624).

Song of Songs has much in common with *From My Diary, July 1914*. Both poems, in similar terms, follow a day from morning to night (a structure of which WO was very fond) and both show a growing adventurousness in working with sounds.

117

l. 5. *voluble leaflets*: an infelicitous phrase! Cf. *From My Diary*, ll. 29-30.

My Shy Hand. p. 72. The final BM draft. Three other drafts use the second and first person pronoun where this and one other use the first and second respectively; and one of these three, sent to Mr Gunston and dated *Aug 29-30th 1917*, is entitled *Sonnet to Beauty*. In Letter 548, WO records that he read to SS three sonnets on 'Beauty' by Leslie Gunston, Olwen Joergens and him-himself. The poem began as an address to Beauty by the poet; as it now stands, it is an address to the reader by Beauty personified.

Written after the meeting with SS, *My Shy Hand* shows a marked advance over WO's previous lyrics. Meaning is still not always very clear but sound is much more consistently controlled; the rich, slow vowels throughout the poem successfully evoke a mood of relaxation and peace.

The Dead-Beat (First Draft). p. 73. An astonishing change from *Song of Songs*! WO has tried immediately to imitate SS's satirical war poems in *The Old Huntsman*. The result is not very successful but it marks the beginning of WO's great period of writing. He has discovered that he can use his own war experience as material for poetry. As in that earlier period of nervous crisis at Dunsden (cf. *On My Songs*), he needs to develop his own style—SS's is not adequate—and his own ideas; all his subsequent poems show how he worked towards, and achieved, that aim.

l. 7. *Caxton Hall*: in Westminster. Used as a wartime recruiting office?

ll. 13 and 16. 'The Emperor yet frowns imperially; and our minis-ters yet wear a ministerial smile' (Letter 370, written from Bor-deaux in August 1915; the ministers are those of the French government, which had moved to the town).

ll. 14-16. Belcher and Bairnsfather were well-known cartoonists, the latter famous for his drawings of the veteran 'Old Bill'; Belloc wrote regularly about the war in *Land and Water*.

The Dead-Beat (Final Draft). p. 74. Despite his gloomy comment that 'the piece as a whole is no good', WO went on working at the poem for at least two months and eight drafts or part-drafts survive. He has tried to act on SS's criticism.

l. 7. *'em*: i.e. not the Germans but *the valiant* back in England who encouraged the man to go out and fight.

l. 9. *Blighty*: Britain (Army slang).

The Letter. p. 75. l. 3. *in the pink*: in very good health. SS's *In the Pink* seems to be WO's inspiration in this poem. The phrase itself was very common in soldiers' letters.

l. 18. *Stand to!*: Stand to arms, prepare for an attack.

The Next War. p. 75. Published anonymously in *The Hydra*, 29th September 1917. The epigraph is the end of SS's *A Letter Home*, addressed to Robert Graves, to which Graves later published a reply. Classified in the Table of Contents as *Cheerfulness* (cf. *Apologia*), the poem shows WO to be perhaps a little too anxious to prove himself acceptable to his new friends.

l. 14. WO had great trouble with this line; it is different in most of the six drafts and there is in addition nearly a whole page of workings for it. EB and *Hydra* have *He wars on Death—for Life; not men—for flags.*

Anthem for Doomed Youth. p. 76. This sonnet was completed by 25th September 1917. There is so much material relevant to its composition that four of the drafts, an early poem, two fragments and some comments are grouped together in Appendix I.

ll. 10-11. Cf. *A maiden with soft eyes like funeral tapers* (Yeats, *The Wanderings of Oisin*).

l. 14. Cf. *At the going down of the sun . . . We will remember them* (Laurence Binyon, *For the Fallen*). WO read Binyon's poem in 1915 and liked it at the time.

Disabled. p. 76. SS showed a draft to Graves, 13th October 1917; an enthusiastic letter from Graves to WO discussing the poem is in *Letters*, Appendix C.

l. 23. *a peg*: usually brandy and soda water (Army slang).

l. 25. *kilts*: the poem has a sexual theme. Men join up to please the women (an early draft is entitled *Why he joined*). This young man was particularly handsome (l. 14) and blood on his legs (l. 21) used to be a sign of virile triumph; the girls wanted him to wear a uniform that would show off his knees. Now he has, through his own choice, lost his knees altogether (l. 10) and the blood on his thigh (l. 20) has left him colourless (l. 17) and impotent (ll. 11-13). The cheers after football (l. 22) have become the futile cheers of patriotic civilians (l. 37).

Conscious. p. 78. A draft is written on the same paper as *Hospital Barge*, which is dated 8th December 1917. SS's *The Death-Bed*, which WO warmly admired, seems to have influenced the poem.

l. 3. Letter 508 records that there were bowls of mayflowers in the Casualty Clearing Station.

l. 12. Cf. the hallucination of blackbird and petals in *Exposure*.

Dulce Et Decorum Est. p. 79. 'Here is a gas poem, done yesterday . . . The famous Latin tag [from Horace's Odes] means of course *It is sweet and meet to die for one's country. Sweet!* And *decorous!*' (Letter 552, ?16th October 1917). WO subtitled the poem *To a Certain Poetess*; she was a Miss Jessie Pope, whose patriotic verse was widely read at the time.

l. 8. This line was actually cancelled by WO but its replacement — *Of gas shells dropping softly that dropped behind* — was obviously not finished.

ll. 15-16. The isolation of these lines stresses their importance. WO is recording one of his shell-shock nightmares. Cf. note on *The Sentry*, l. 23.

ll. 23-24. These lines replace an earlier attempt:

> *And think how, once, his head was like a bud,*
> *Fresh as a country rose, and keen, and young,—*

The Chances. p. 80. CDL and EB follow what appears to be the penultimate draft. The final draft makes a number of improvements, including the omission of the wholly superfluous third and fourth lines, the substitution of *One lad* for the ambiguous *T'other* (l. 10), better punctuation and a reduction in the number of abbreviations.

l. 3. Infantry assaults were launched 'over the top' of the trench parapets.

l. 8. *Scuppered*: here used to mean taken prisoner by the Germans (*Fritz*).

l. 14. *a blighty*: a wound serious enough for the soldier to be sent back to Britain.

Soldier's Dream. p. 80. Sent to Osbert Sitwell in summer 1918: an earlier version, which has *a man from U.S.A.* instead of God and Michael, WO described as 'the last piece from Craiglockhart' (i.e. October 1917).

l. 7. *Michael*: the archangel in command of the heavenly armies.

Inspection. p. 81. The first of two drafts is entitled *Dirt* (see note on *A Terre*).

l. 7 *damnéd spot*: *Macbeth* V, i. The blood on Lady Macbeth's hand is, of course, a symbol of her guilt and she tries in vain to wash it away.

l. 15. *white-washed*: before a high-ranking officer inspects an Army camp the men are sometimes sent round white-washing every possible object—a superficial cleaning done to impress authority, and one which is the target of much Army sarcasm.

Asleep. p. 81. One of the four drafts is entitled *Lines on a soldier whom shrapnel killed asleep*; another is dated *Nov. 14 1917*. The poem 'came from the Winchester Downs, as I crossed the long backs of the downs after leaving you . . . I could almost see the dead lying about in the hollows of the downs' (Letter 561).

l. 6. *aborted*: one draft originally read *Of frustrated life like child within him leaping*.

Apologia pro Poemate Meo. p. 82. 'A defence of my poem.' Titles on earlier drafts: *The Unsaid, Apologia pro Poema Disconsolatia Mea*. The 1920 edition corrected the Latin grammar. WO seems to be answering a criticism that a poem, or possibly his poetry in general, is 'disconsolate'; he includes *Apologia* under *Cheerfulness* in the Table of Contents. (Graves, e.g., wrote in December 1917: 'For God's sake cheer up and write more optimistically—The war's not ended yet but a poet should have a spirit above wars'. It is tempting to see the poem as a direct answer to this letter, but one draft is dated *November 1917*.) WO's defence of his gloominess is that, although he has indeed found cause for cheerfulness at the Front, he has not tried to describe it in case the people at home might think that soldiers do not need pity.

The first four stanzas, using Christian terminology, describe the ecstasy that is part of war experience—a state in which the mind surges above horror to a quasi-religious mode of perception. (Cf. 'I lost all my earthly faculties, and fought like an angel', Letter 662, early October 1918.) Stanzas 5 and 6 describe the comradeship of soldiers in metaphors of tying together, in which military methods of binding are substituted for images traditional in love poetry of Joy's ribbon, kisses and the bonds of interchanged looks. WO is remembering poems by Graves and Leslie Gunston. The seventh stanza is a development of *Conscious*, l. 12.

ll. 1 and 9. *I, too*: why *too*? DSRW makes a convincing connection with Graves' *Two Fusiliers* (in *Men Who March Away*, ed. I. M. Parsons, p. 168) which WO read when it was published in November 1917. Graves describes his friendship with another Fusilier, no doubt SS, and provides WO with some of his images:

> *By wire and wood and stake we're bound . . .*
> *. . . by the wet bond of blood,*
> *By friendship, blossoming from mud,*
> *By Death: we faced him, and we found*
> *Beauty in Death,*
> *In dead men breath.*

l. 8. An early draft has *For God forgets Christ then and blesses murder. God* in l. 1 should be understood in some such sense as 'Christ-like devotion'. For another contrast between God the Father and God the Son, cf. *Soldier's Dream.*

ll. 18-20. Cf. Leslie Gunston's poem *L'Amour*, also published in November 1917, beginning:

> *Love is the binding of souls together,*
> *The binding of lips, the binding of eyes.*

Hospital Barge at Cérisy. p. 83. MS dated *Dec. 8 1917.* Written after 'a Saturday night revel in *The Passing of Arthur*' (letter quoted in EB; not in *Letters*). 'I sailed in a steam-tug about 6 miles down the Canal . . . The scenery was such as I never saw or dreamed of since I read the *Faerie Queene.* Just as in the Winter when I woke up lying on the burning cold snow I fancied I must have died & been pitch-forked into the Wrong Place, so, yesterday, it was not more difficult to imagine that my dusky barge was wending up to Avalon, and the peace of Arthur, and where Lancelot heals him of his grievous wound. But the Saxon is not broken, as we could very well hear last night. Later, a real thunderstorm did its best to seem terrible, and quite failed' (Letter 509, 10 May 1917).

ll. 13-14. King Arthur, after being wounded in battle with the Saxons, was carried to Avalon in a barge, accompanied by mourning women.

> *Long stood Sir Bedivere*
> *Revolving many memories, till the hull*
> *Look'd one black dot against the verge of dawn,*
> *And on the mere the wailing died away.*
>   (Tennyson, *The Passing of Arthur*)

Beauty. p. 84. Possibly not begun as a war poem (cf. some earlier lines given in CDL and my note on *My Shy Hand*); the work given here seems to be a new start but it was not taken further. l. 2. 'The man crouching shoulder to shoulder to me gets a beautiful round hole deep in his biceps. I am nothing so fortunate . . .' (Letter 503). The wound is a *beauty* because it is a blighty— cf. *The Chances*, l. 14, n.

l. 8. *Kant*: Immanuel Kant (1724-1804), the German philosopher.

I saw his round mouth's crimson. p. 84. Entitled *Fragment* by EB and CDL but the MS, though untitled and a half-sheet, is a fair copy and seems a complete poem. Again, this is a single image, one of WO's most startling conceits: the features of a dying man, who is presumably bleeding at the mouth, are compared to a sunset sky.

As bronze may be much beautified. p. 85. There is no sign of any further stanzas but the third, despite much revision, was never finished. The pararhymes and the subterranean imagery may suggest a 1918 date.

Cramped in that funnelled hole. p. 85. Part of a very rough sheet of jotted lines and phrases. The ancient symbol of the Hell-mouth is taken literally: the shell-crater's jagged edge, revealed in the dawn light, is the teeth; the mud at the bottom is the phlegm in the throat—another nightmarish physical image. WO had always been interested in ideas to do with hell and descents into the underworld, as is shown by several unpublished pre-war poems as well as such war poems as *Strange Meeting*, *Mental Cases*, and *Spring Offensive*.

Miners. p. 87. 'Wrote a poem on the Colliery Disaster: but I get mixed up with the War at the end. It is short, but oh! sour' (quoted by EB; not in *Letters*). A pit explosion at the Podmore Hall Colliery, Halmerend, on 12th January 1918, killed about 140 men and boy miners. WO wrote the poem in half an hour (Letter 587) and sent it at once to *The Nation*, in which it was published on 26th January, the first of WO's poems to appear in a national periodical. Leslie Gunston wrote soon afterwards to say that the rhymes offended his 'musical ear'; WO replied 'I suppose I am doing in poetry what the advanced composers are doing in music. I am not satisfied with either' (Letter 589).

The coal is expected to tell of its prehistoric origins—WO was always interested in geology—but instead it speaks of the sufferings of miners, and the fossils in it seem to be of human bones.

The image of the dark pit (darkness, as always, stimulating WO's imagination) suggests the trenches; the miners become soldiers, hewing out peace for the comfort of later ages but not for their own. The fuel of peace, as only Death knows, is the bodies of dead men. The Halmerend disaster thus becomes an image of the war and also, perhaps, of a social system which obliges some men to risk death so that others can be prosperous. It is not surprising that WO's poetry has appealed to the socialist movement.

Rhyming devices are used as part of the stanza pattern. In stanza 4, for example, there are the sequences *murmuring-mine-moans-men, their-there-air, wry-Writing*—sounds which, placed at careful intervals, together suggest moans and agonised gasps of pain. The pararhymes descend in pitch in some pairs (*simmer/summer, groaned/ground*, etc.) and support the deep-sounding syllables of the later stanzas and the sighing *s* and *w* sounds of the early ones, to achieve an extraordinarily sombre tone.

l. 8. *fawns*: WO may have meant *fauns*.

l. 19. The only surviving draft gives an alternative line: *Many the muscled bodies charred*.

The Last Laugh. p. 88. Both drafts are given because they show how WO transposed full rhyme into pararhyme. The final draft was sent to Osbert Sitwell in summer 1918 and the first to Mrs Owen on 18th February 1918.

Insensibility. p. 89. WO records being satisfied with an Ode he has just written in March 1918. This must be *Insensibility* which is a 'Pindaric' Ode characterised by irregular rhymes and line lengths (cf. Wordsworth's *Ode: Intimations of Immortality*). WO considers various categories of people who have become insensible to the horrors of war: soldiers who have suffered so much that they can no longer feel for their fellows (I) or for themselves (II); who have lost their powers of imagination (III); who have been sent home wounded or on leave and can forget (IV); or who have not been *trained* to think ahead (IV). These men are fortunate and are contrasted with *We wise* (V), the poets who have been *trained* and who find that their imaginations fill with blood every time they think. How should they set about writing their poetry (l. 42)? They must learn the insensibility of the common soldier, approaching their task in a similarly dispassionate, objective way; then, like him, they will be able to *sing* and to keep their imaginations under control. WO expounds his new understanding of how he can write about his subject without relapsing into nightmare and mental chaos. His final category of insensible people is that of the *dullards* (VI) who have never experienced battle and who feel nothing for the sufferers; for this callousness there can be no excuse. These people have made themselves immune *by choice* not only to the miseries of war but also to everything that is tragic in the human condition.

l. 5. 'They are dying again at Beaumont Hamel, which already in 1916 was cobbled with skulls' (Letter 605, March 1918).

l. 8. *fooling*: cf. *Six o'clock in Princes Street*, l. 5.

l. 55. *mourns*: WO wrote *mourns*, then crossed it out and substituted *moans*. *Moans* provides a pararhyme, avoids repetition, and gives the sequence *mean-immune-moans-man-mourns-many*; but there is a strongly held critical opinion (which the present editor does not altogether share) that it is too narrow and physical a word and that WO would have changed it back again to *mourns*. If this view is correct, it is strange that WO did not make the change, since he had seven months in which to do so. There is an excellent analysis of the sound effects in this stanza in DSRW, pp. 120-122.

l. 56. Cf. *Between the loud stream and the trembling stars* (Tennyson, *Oenone*, 215).

Exposure. p. 91. WO dates the final draft *Feb 1916*, which is clearly incorrect since the experience described occurred in February 1917 (see Letter 482, p. 63). It seems unlikely that the finished poem could even date from so early in 1917, though SS and a *Letters* footnote have suggested that it does. The final MS is written on the same paper as a minor poem almost certainly dating from September 1918; but WO quotes the refrain *Nothing happens* in April 1918 (Letter 612) and the poem appears under that title in the Table of Contents. In fact, *Exposure* is likely to have been revised over a very long period; the MSS certainly support such a view—there are four large sheets densely covered with rough work in addition to the final draft, which is itself heavily revised.

Because he is describing a seemingly endless experience, in which *nothing happens* except hallucination, WO uses a monotonous refrain and an exceptionally long line, made even longer by slow, heavy stresses and strong punctuation; the approximate rhymes thus occur at widely spaced intervals so that a drawn-out, melancholy echo runs through the poem.

l. 1. An ironic echo of Keats (*Ode to the Nightingale*, l. 1).

l. 3. *salient*: the Line at places jutted out into enemy territory; at such 'salients' fighting tended to be fiercest.

l. 14. *gray*: the German army, which, like the dawn, attacked from the east, was uniformed in field gray.

st. 5. As elsewhere, the sounds parallel the experience described. (Death by exposure can be preceded by hallucination and a sense of drowsy warmth.) The stealthy *f* sounds suggest the gentle, murderous touch of the snow; soft, sleepy words follow (*dreams, dazed, deep, drowsed*). The trenches seem to become ditches, the flakes petals, and a blackbird appears with busy, cheerful noises (*grassier, blossoms, fusses*, and the short *i* of *ditches, Littered, trickling*) —a vividness of sound to illustrate the vividness of the hallucination. The almost imperceptible change from cold to warmth is paralleled by the closeness in sound of *snow-dazed* and *sun-dozed*. Then the refrain changes as the men realise that they may be dying. This brilliant transition in words from battlefield to countryside has something of a film-maker's technique in it; perhaps the producer of the film of *O What A Lovely War* had it in mind in his final sequence when a character is killed and drifts, as though in a dream, into a rural landscape.

l. 26. *glozed*; perhaps this is a combination of 'glowing' and 'glazed' but 'glazed' would have been more usual. DSRW suggests WO wanted a full rhyme to represent the completeness of home life. With this stanza, cf. the song: *Keep the home fires burning . . . Though your lads are far away they dream of home.*

st. 7. Perhaps evidence that this is in origin an early 1917 poem. The sacrificial imagery harks back to *Greater Love* and the seasonal metaphor even further to *1914*. Cf. Introduction, p. 37, and part of a very early war poem, *The Ballad of Purchase Money*, quoted in EB's Memoir:

> *Fair days are yet left for the old*
> *And children's cheeks are ruddy,*
> *Because the good lads' limbs lie cold*
> *And their brave cheeks are bloody.*

l. 36. *this*: CDL follows EB in giving *His* here but admits that the MS almost certainly reads *this*. Like *mourns* for *moans* in *Insensibility*, *His* has strong support but I am sure WO meant the word to be read as this. If WO did write *His*, he meant that the frost is sent by God and that the men suffer because God wills them to. There is a possible parallel in the *Inferno*, where Dante finds sinners condemned by God to stand in a lake of ice—they can neither see nor weep because their eyes are frozen over (cf. *All their eyes are ice*, l. 39).

st. 8. WO worked particularly hard on this stanza; there was to have been a ninth stanza, continuing the house image, but he abandoned this and in the eighth struggled with further house imagery, comparing bodies to plaster and faces to bricks; this obviously wouldn't do but it suggested *picks and shovels*. Eventually, at a late stage, the burial party emerged as a solution.

l. 38. Previous editors give *shovels in their shaking*; I cannot find *their* in MS.

The Show. p. 92. Slang for a battle (cf. *The Chances*, l. 1), but a picture-show is also implied. The lines from the non-acting version of Yeats's *The Shadowy Waters* and WO's vision make a bitter juxtaposition; Yeats's languid, elegant gods occupy themselves in making picture-shows by breathing on *the mirror of the world*. WO sees the battlefield not as a smooth mirror but as the maggot-infested face of a gigantic corpse. The image is sustained throughout the poem—*sweats, pocks, scabs, beard, warts, mouths, wounds*. The metaphor and the poet's high vantage point may in part derive from a wide variety of literary sources—Hardy's *The Dynasts*, Barbusse's *Under Fire*, Tailhade, even certain passages of H. G. Wells—but no other writer has made it so appalling or so detailed. Cf. Letter 481, p. 63.

'I looked back and saw the ground all crawling and wormy with wounded bodies' (Letter 510, May 1917, referring to Fayet). In April 1918, when the German advance was causing fighting over the same ground, WO wrote that he was 'haunted by the vision of the lands about St Quentin crawling with wounded' (Letter 608). *The Show* may well have been written that April at Ripon. Its MS is very similar to that of *S.I.W.*; the two poems may be contemporary. Perhaps WO was reading Yeats's plays at the time.

Rather than use a rigid stanza form, WO treats each sentence as a separate stanza, making a jagged pattern which is further structured by means of a variety of rhyming. Like the 'show' itself, the poem is harsh and out of tune but not merely chaotic.

l. 10. *slimy*: the details of the image are worked out with WO's usual thoroughness. Caterpillars can leave a slimy track; the bottoms of the communication trenches were slimy with mud.

l. 14. *foul openings*: many war memoirs record the intolerable stench of the dug-outs.

l. 17. The caterpillars are files of men armed with bayonets (*spines*), *brown* in British khaki or *gray* in the German uniform.

l. 18. *green fields*: writers of the time used to point out that if one could have viewed the Front from the air one would have seen how it ran like a strip of mud through lush countryside; into that strip, men and materials poured unceasingly. The *migrants* are aiming for the *mire*, the link in sound emphasising the link in sense—almost a pun (cf. *wry-Writhing* in *Miners*, *pallor-pall* in *Anthem for Doomed Youth*, *eyes-ice* in *Exposure*).

l. 29. *my head*: the poet has been killed while leading a file of his men; the file has not reached shelter in time. He is thus guilty not only in a general sense as in *Mental Cases* but also in a particular sense, because he has failed to lead his men to safety. Was WO helpless with shell-shock, leaving his men exposed and leaderless, when he lay for days in that 'hole' at Fayet?

S.I.W. p. 93. Military abbreviation for Self-Inflicted Wound. The epigraph is from Yeats's play *The King's Threshold*. At some late stage, WO revised *S.I.W.* very hastily in pencil. On the back he scribbled:

This study consists of four pieces
   I The Prologue—a satire
   II The Incident—narrative
   III The Apology—a poem
   IV The Epilogue—a cynicism

and then he inserted the four headings into the poem, altering them as in the printed text. At the same time, he altered the third section to increase its 'poetic' quality and to sharpen the contrast between its style and that of the sections before and after it, leaving it largely illegible; the CDL text is as near WO's intentions as we are likely to get.

l. 10. *Y.M. Hut*: hostel for troops run by the Young Men's Christian Association.

l. 11. *butt*: the flat shoulder-piece of a rifle.

ll. 15-16. *Courage . . . rain*: just as earlier Romantic poets had compared psychological processes to the landscape, so WO takes images to describe a soldier's mental state from the environment of war. Cf. *Apologia pro Poemate Meo* for some more complex examples.

l. 37. *smiling*: one of WO's many references to laughter. Tim was smiling because he was pleased, but also because the rifle had blown his mouth open.

A Terre. p. 95. An expanded version of an earlier poem called *Wild with All Regrets* (cf. *wild with all regret;/O Death in Life, the days that are no more.* Tennyson, *Tears, Idle Tears*). The first poem is dated *Dec 5 1917* and is dedicated to SS; *A Terre* was being worked on in April 1918 and must have been finished by the summer.

l. 8. It used to be customary to place coins on the eyelids of a corpse to keep them closed.

l. 30. *dirt*: WO plays on the word. Dirt can be dust or muck to be cleared away; it can also be soil. Flesh rots into earth (hence the title of the poem) and can therefore also be described as dirt. Cf. also *clay* in *Futility* and *dirt* in *Inspection*.

l. 37. *existences*. Editors have preferred this cancelled word to *lives*, WO's final version.

l. 44.   *He is made one with Nature: there is heard*
   His voice in all her music, from the moan
   Of thunder, to the song of night's sweet bird;
   He is a presence to be felt and known
   In darkness and in light, from herb and stone,
   Spreading itself where'er that Power may move
   Which has withdrawn his being to its own . . .
                         (Shelley, *Adonais* XLII)

l. 47. '*Pushing up daisies*': common military slang. The phrase reminds us that this poem describes 'the philosophy of many soldiers'. By using Tommies' language, WO is able to relate Shelley's statement to the theme of earth; a dead man becomes earth and is incorporated into plants, a literal version of becoming *one with nature*. Once again, WO interprets war in Romantic terms.

ll. 49-51. Unsatisfactorily obscure. Cf. *I told him with a sympathetic grin/That Germans boil dead soldiers down for fat* (SS, *The Tombstone Maker*). SS refers to a belief widely held at the time. Since the officer is to become *grain*, he might just as well be eaten in soup. Presumably we are meant to complete the sentence with some such phrase as 'if the war goes on much longer'.

ll. 56-65. The speaker realises that the idea of becoming one with the plants is only a *poor comfort*: plants are as vulnerable as bodies to artillery fire: but it is his only hope. Meanwhile, in his present state of being less than half-alive, his *soul* or *spirit* does not seem to inhabit his own body but to exist in the sympathy in his friend's mind. This sympathy being the only spiritual fact he can still recognise, he asks his friend, in the last two lines, to keep his soul, until his body dies, by continuing to sympathise. After that, perhaps, he may *grow a soul* after he has grown fronds and become a plant. The word *jest* (l. 58) perhaps indicates that the friend has laughed at the oddness of the philosophy being expounded.

Arms and the Boy. p. 97. A copy sent to Osbert Sitwell is dated 3rd May 1918. Classified by WO under *Protest — The unnaturalness of weapons*. Geoffrey Matthews points out (*Stand*, IV, 3) that the image of the hungry bayonet comes from Shelley (*Mask of Anarchy*, LXXVII).

The Send-Off. p. 97. There are 5½ drafts, covering a period of several months in spring 1918; WO took much care over the form of this poem and the final version is one of his most accomplished achievements. The stanza pattern given here differs slightly from CDL: WO's revisions have partially obscured two of the seven spaces between stanzas in the final draft, so that editors have seen six stanzas where WO, in my opinion, intended eight.

l. 3. *grimly gay*: one of several paradoxes. The signals *nod* yet are *unmoved*; the tramp is moved (*sorry*) but *stands* still, is *casual* but stares *hard*; the flowers, meant for good luck, suggest a funeral.

l. 10. The men are victims of a conspiracy: the lamp *winks* and the signals *nod*; and they are sent away *like wrongs hushed up*.

Futility. p. 98. Published in *The Nation* in June 1918.

l. 3. *At home*: two earlier drafts have *In Wales*. This is one of several examples in WO's later poems of his avoidance of proper names (cf. his Preface).

l. 7. *The kind old sun*: a familiar phrase, suggesting—ironically under the circumstances—that the sun has been an old friend. This relationship between sun and soldier appears again in *Spring Offensive*. *know*: a full rhyme with *snow*, a pararhyme with *now*, and an assonantal pair with *unsown*; *unsown* in its turn is a pararhyme with *sun, sun* is linked with *once* and *once* is a half-rhyme with *France*—an intricate pattern, mingling harmony and dissonance.

l. 9. The local imagery of the preceding lines is now paralleled on a universal scale: *fields unsown* become the *clays* of the whole earth; *this snow* becomes the coldness of the lifeless planet before the end of the Ice Age.

Mental Cases. p. 98. WO referred to this as 'my terrific poem (at present) called "The Deranged" ' (Letter 622); the final draft, written in early summer 1918, he headed *Mental Cases,* then *The Aliens,* and then, preferring the ironic understatement of the official term (cf. *Disabled, S.I.W.*), went back firmly to *Mental Cases.* No doubt the poem contains memories of Craiglockhart, but much of the descriptive material comes from a remarkable MS headed *Purgatorial Passions* which probably dates from 1915 or 1916 and is a vision of the damned in hell (cf. l. 2). WO had read Dante, and *Mental Cases* is given a Dantesque structure: a visitor in hell asks for information and is answered. He sees men who have witnessed *multitudinous murders* and who are condemned *always* (l. 15) to see the horrors they once saw, as the damned suffer eternal torment.

The poem's vocabulary is deliberately harsh and contorted, with hard *c* and *s* sounds predominating (*rock, skulls', wicked, stroke, panic, chasms, sockets,* etc.), suggesting the awkward movements and inarticulate sounds of the madmen.

ll. 27-8. WO suddenly insists that he bears some of the blame; cf. the last lines of *The Show. Brother* must refer to the speaker of the first stanza (a brother poet, as Dante was to Virgil?).

The Kind Ghosts. p. 99. The only MS, dated *30/7/18,* shows WO at work on sound effects: in the first stanza, for example, he marks each *s, st, l* and *d* to indicate alliteration.

l. 11. *hecatombs*: 'great public sacrifices' (OED); but WO seems to use the word, incorrectly, to mean simply 'tombs'. Did he intend 'catacombs'?

The Calls. p. 100. Printed as two separate poems by EB; DSRW made the connection.

l. 12. i.e. 'I sing the amen of religion in the same meaningless, repetitive way that pigeons make their calls'. Or 'I sing the amen of my religion, which is the same religion as that of pigeons' (cf. *I learn from the daisy*).

ll. 18-19. *food-hog*: a reference to 'the stinking Leeds and Bradford War-profiteers' (Letter 643)? *Eat less bread* may have been a slogan in the Food Economy Campaign of 1917-18.

st. 5. WO made two attempts at a fourth line for this stanza: he wrote *I've had my fill*, then *Here I've no rime that's proper* and then cancelled both.

l. 28. This line possibly records WO's decision of late July 1918 to return to the Front; the stanza makes it clear that he will return because he, unlike the men, has both the skill and the will *To speak of their distress*.

Strange Meeting. p. 102. Discussed at length in the Introduction. There is one final draft and an earlier one, and five pages of work related to ll. 28-39 inclusive (see note below). The poem is in WO's Table of Contents and so is likely to have been written by August 1918 at the latest. Like *Mental Cases*, the poem is a vision in Hell.

l. 1. *out of battle*: originally *from my dug-out*.

ll. 9-11. The theme of perceiving the truth by looking at a suffering face is presumably a deliberate echo of Keats's sight of the face of Moneta in *The Fall of Hyperion*. Cf. WO's use of a similar image in *Storm*.

l. 25. *the pity war distilled*: originally *the one thing war distilled*.

l. 29. WO seems to foresee the solidarity of the totalitarian state and the retreat from civilised values that occurred in so many countries after the war.

l. 36. *Even with truths that lie*: originally *Even the wells I sank*.

l. 39. A variant line, quoted below, suggests that Christ is referred to here. Cf. 'and his sweat was as it were great drops of blood falling down to the ground' (*Luke* xxii, 44). Cf. also Shelley, *Prometheus Unbound*, I, 564-5. The task of the non-violent poet is a redeeming, Christlike one. WO does not suggest here, however, that the poet who fights and dies is also a redeemer; on the contrary, such a poet has abandoned his task and damned himself. The ideas expressed in *Greater Love* and other poems no longer have any validity.

l. 40. Originally *I was a German conscript and your friend*.

l. 44. This final line was pencilled in, with its four dots, as an afterthought; but later WO inked it in. There is some evidence that he intended to continue the poem further but decided not to and added this line instead.

Strange Meeting Variants. Variant readings given above are all cancelled work in the final draft, which is heavily revised. The other drafts seem to be work for a separate poem which was later incorporated into *Strange Meeting*. It began as pararhymed couplets and appears to be an address to a companion, much on the lines of Cythna's speech to Laon in *The Revolt of Islam* II (and see stanza XLII for WO's *wells* image?). There is no trace of the cavern of *Strange Meeting*, nor of the recognition theme nor of the hopelessness; the speech is an exhortation to positive future action. Beauty and Truth are shared by the two characters. All the drafts begin with versions of:

> *Earth's wheels run oiled with blood. Forget we that.*
> *Let us turn back to beauty and to thought.*
>
> *Beauty is* $\frac{yours}{mine}$ *and* $\frac{you}{I}$ *have mastery*
>
> *Wisdom is* $\frac{mine}{yours}$ *and* $\frac{I}{you}$ *have mystery.*
> *We two will stay behind and keep our troth*
> *Let us lie out and keep the open truth.*

There follows substantially the same material as in *Strange Meeting*, and then the two characters are seen as *pitchers, falling* from men now but eventually to be raised up again to be men's *filling*,

> *Even from wells we sunk too deep for war*
> { *And filled by brows that bled where no wounds were*
> { *Even as One who bled where no wounds were.*

The Sentry. p. 103. There is a rough draft of ll. 1-16 apparently dating from summer 1918; but the final draft is similar to that of *Smile, smile, smile* (which is dated September). WO sent a copy to SS on 22nd September, asking him to confer a title on it and suggesting *The Blind*, so that the present title could be SS's. WO is remembering a single incident of 18 months before in considerable detail—see Letter 480, p. 61.

l. 23. WO was still suffering from 'war dreams'. The sea imagery (*squids', flound'ring*) is reminiscent of that other nightmare passage in *Dulce et Decorum Est*, ll. 13-16.

l. 28. *one*; WO himself (see his letter).

l. 36. *lights*: what lights? Candles? Or the lights of faith and hope? Cf. Sir Edward Grey's famous remark, 'The lamps are going out all over Europe'.

Smile, smile, smile. p. 106. The song, popular among the troops, went:

> *What's the use of worrying?*
> *It never was worth while,*
> *So, pack up your troubles in your old kit-bag*
> *And smile, smile, smile.*

Letter 660, p. 105, explains the genesis of this poem. It is the last we can positively date. Clemenceau's speech to the Senate appeared in full in *The Times*, 19th September 1918; it is a characteristic piece of inflated rhetoric, making that insistence on total victory which so enraged the troops in the final stages of the war (and which prolonged the fighting and caused WO's death). The poem quotes from this paragraph:

> 'All are worthy of victory, because they will know how to honour it. Yet, however, in the ancient spot where sit the fathers of the Republic we should be untrue to ourselves if we forgot that the greatest glory will be to those splendid *poilus* [common soldiers] who will see confirmed by history the titles of nobility which they themselves have earned. At the present moment they ask for nothing more than to be allowed to complete the great work which will assure them of immortality. What do they want and what do you? To keep on fighting victoriously until the moment when the enemy will understand there is no possible negotiation between crime and right.'

l. 20. *secret*: explained in the parenthesis. WO refers to the 'Two Nations'; the nation of men who know the truth about war is mostly dead (*under France*) and the survivors *never speak* their secret to the other nation, those who have never experienced war.

Spring Offensive. p. 108. WO sent a draft of ll. 1-17 to SS on 22nd September 1918 with a note 'Is this worth going on with?/I don't want to write anything to which a soldier would say *No Compris!*' The only BM draft is complete to l. 37; the first revisions were in ink. Then WO revised the poem, and added the last stanza, in rapid pencil. Finally, he went back to the beginning and started revising in ink—but he did not live to finish the job. Some lines remain hard to decipher. CDL and EB give a row of asterisks between stanzas 5 and 6 but this, though dramatic, does not seem to be justified by the MS. The poem is discussed in the Introduction.

WO was involved in the Allied 'spring offensive' in 1917, being one of a party that captured the village of Fayet. He was in action without relief for 12 days and emerged with shell-shock. For some of his comments on this experience, see Letters 505 and 510, pp. 65-66.

l. 5. DSRW assumes that the poem is set at dawn; it seems more likely to be late afternoon. The sun is above the ridge, lighting the long valley up which the men have come and leaving the hillside in shade; the sky ahead, above the ridge, has a harsh reflecting glare (*glass*) with no depth to it. The world seems to end there. At no point does WO mention the hidden enemy.

l. 6. *the end of the world*: an ambitious and sudden image, warning us that the poem is going to deal with war in cosmic terms. Robert Nichols, friend of Graves and SS and a celebrated war poet in his day, quoted this line in the Introduction to his *Anthology of War Poetry* (1943) and said that 'if that be not great poetry I do not know wherein greatness in this art consists'.

l. 10. *bodies'*: as opposed to *souls* in the next line. Cf. ll. 20 and 40.

l. 15. *blessed with gold*: damp petals have stuck to the men's boots. The image originated from a family ramble years before (*Journey from Obscurity*, I, 176-7)

l. 17. *hands*: WO substituted this for *arms*, perhaps because arms do not clutch; but l. 21 loses its rhyme.

l. 18. WO did not complete this line; the first half, *All their strange day*, is cancelled.

l. 26. *his*: i.e. the sun's.

l. 27. *raced*: the troops walked slowly at Fayet, but WO wants to suggest the 'exultation' and excitement of the moment.

l. 30. *sudden cups*: a brilliant image. The word *cups* suggests not only shell-holes but also *buttercup* (l. 14) and chalices, cups which are used in the Mass to contain the wine which is both a blessing (cf. *blessed with gold*) and sacrificial blood. Having refused the offered blessing of communion with the natural order, the men have become victims sacrificed to an outraged Nature.

l. 33. *last high place*: another reference to sacrifice—hilltop sacrificial altars were known in ancient times as 'high places'.

l. 34. Very heavily revised in MS. CDL follows EB in what he admits to be almost certainly an incorrect version of the line. WO first wrote *Leapt to unseen bullets or went up*. Among the confused revisions which followed, two possible readings could be *In the even rapture of bullets, went up* or, as Professor Welland suggests, *Breasted the surf of bullets, or went up.* EB seems to have read *surf* as *swift* but I retain his version for want of an agreed alternative.

l. 37. *Some*: i.e. some of the people at home. There is an ironical stress on this word.

l. 45. *cool, peaceful*: as opposed to *the hot blast* in l. 35. The landscape, having purged itself of its attackers, has resumed its serenity. Perhaps twilight has fallen.

APPENDIX I

OWEN'S PREFACE AND TABLE OF CONTENTS

Preface

This book is not about heroes. English Poetry is not yet fit to speak of them.

Nor is it about deeds, or lands, nor anything about glory, honour, might, majesty, dominion, or power, except War.

5 Above all I am not concerned with Poetry.

My subject is War, and the pity of War.

The Poetry is in the pity.

Yet these elegies are to this generation in no sense consolatory. They may be to the next. All a poet can do today is warn. That

10 is why the true Poets must be truthful.

If I thought the letter of this book would last, I might have used proper names; but if the spirit of it survives—survives Prussia—my ambition and those names will have achieved themselves fresher fields than Flanders . . .

[The Table of Contents]

138

NOTES

Preface. WO drafted this Preface, together with the Table of Contents, at some time in the summer of 1918. The Preface is heavily revised, especially in the last two paragraphs, and is obviously unfinished. It was intended for a small volume exclusively of war poems to have been published in 1919. It is possible that WO later abandoned the idea of such a volume (see Additional Note A).

l. 5. *Poetry*: WO seems to mean that he is not concerned with writing poetry for poetry's sake.

l. 13. *Prussia*: probably WO uses the term here in the same sense that he used it in his letters, to indicate militarism in any country.

Table of Contents. A list of war poems only—the *elegies* referred to in the Preface—categorised with some care. WO begins with *Miners*, his only poem then known to the public, and nine other poems under the general heading of *Protest*. (*Sonnet* is no doubt the *Artillery* sonnet; *Aliens* was a draft title for *Mental Cases*.) A miscellaneous section follows (perhaps the classifications in the lower right-hand corner were possible labels for some of its contents) and three poems linked as *Description*. *The Draft* was a provisional title for *The Send-Off*; *Nothing happens* must be *Exposure*, a clue that that poem was not yet finalised; *The Light* may be *The Sentry*. The third section, *Grief*, contains five poems describing the pity of war (*Ode* is almost certainly *Insensibility*). *Strange Meeting* is in a section on its own. The last section is apparently *Philosophy*; DSRW suggests that the final title may be another name for *Disabled*. Of these three poems, two tackle the question of life after death and one the sexual motives in fighting.

WO's list of *Motives* is interesting, as is the column headed *Doubtful*. *A ponderous day* is perhaps *The Unreturning* (an early draft begins *A ponderous night*); *Heaven* is another title for *To a Comrade in Flanders* and *The Seed* for *1914*. These are all early poems, not based on war experience and the hard thinking that began at Craiglockhart; so it is interesting to find *Greater Love* and *The End* there as well, two poems which critics sometimes treat as works of major importance. *Greater Love* appears twice; perhaps the second entry refers to *At a Calvary near the Ancre*.

The Table may therefore contain all WO's published war poems except *Le Christianisme*, a lightweight piece probably never intended for publication; *The Calls*, too personal and incomplete for inclusion; and *Spring Offensive, Smile, smile, smile* and *The Kind Ghosts*, all written after the Table was drawn up. The date of that drawing up must have been somewhere between 15 June, when WO was still referring to *Mental Cases* by its first draft title of *The Deranged*, and 30 July, the date of *The Kind Ghosts*.

APPENDIX II
ADDITIONAL NOTES

A. OWEN'S PLANS FOR THE FUTURE

(i) *Publication*

According to Edmund Blunden, as early as 1913 Owen was planning a collection of verse, though neither the title—*Minor Poems—in Minor Keys—by a Minor*—nor the plan can have been very serious. A note in the British Museum suggests he amused himself at the Casualty Clearing Station in 1917 with a further scheme: the projected volume was to have had a cover in his favourite colour, purple.

At Craiglockhart, Sassoon at first advised Owen against early publishing, but in the autumn changed his mind after hearing his latest work and urged him to prepare typescripts at once for Heinemann, who had already published books by Sassoon and Graves. Owen does not seem to have acted on this advice immediately, but he sent *Anthem for Doomed Youth* to *The Nation*; the editor was impressed but did not print the poem. In January, however, *The Nation* accepted *Miners*. Owen was pleased with this achievement and, since the periodical attracted a discriminating readership, his reputation grew a little. At about the same time, he entered for a competition run by *The Bookman* for writers actively involved in the war effort. There were prizes for both ballads and lyrics and he tried for both; Leslie Gunston entered a lyric. The ballad was unplaced (it probably survives as one of a group of unpublished ballads in the British Museum) but the lyric, a version of *Song of Songs*, won a consolation prize and was printed in the May 1918 edition. On 15th June 1918, *Futility* and *Hospital Barge* were published in *The Nation*. These, apart from two pieces which Owen published himself in *The Hydra* at Craiglockhart (*Song of Songs* and *The Next War*), were the only poems published in his lifetime.

At Ripon, in May 1918, Owen began definite plans for publishing his collected poems in 1919, with the help of Robert Ross, who was an associate of Heinemann's. In July, the Sitwells asked for poems for their anthology, *Wheels*; Owen sent some, but probably too late for the 1918 edition. Seven poems appeared in *Wheels* in 1919. A footnote in the *Letters* refers to a note by Owen of what is apparently a *complete* list of his poems and also a list of people to whom a volume containing all his poems could be sent (Tailhade, Bennet, Wells, Yeats and Robert Nichols are included). Two possible titles— *With Lightning and With Music* (cf. Shelley, *Adonais*, XII) and *English Elegies* (cf. Tennyson, *English Idyls*)—are rejected in favour of *Disabled and Other Poems*.

The Preface and Table of Contents in the British Museum have already been noted. The volume to which they would have belonged was, unlike *Disabled and Other Poems*, to have excluded poems not about the war. Neither the Preface nor the Table of Contents are much more than rough notes: if Owen could be shown to have abandoned them in favour of his scheme for a complete collection, we should have that much less reason to call him a mere 'war poet'.

(ii) *Writing*

Speculation as to what Owen would have written had he survived has only a handful of facts to go on. A footnote in the *Letters* (p. 551) quotes a note written at Ripon on 5 May 1918 in which Owen lists four projects: *Collected Poems 1919*, blank verse plays, *Perseus* and *Idylls in Prose*. The plays were to be on old Welsh themes on the models of Tennyson and Yeats, whose plays are on old English and old Irish themes respectively—did Owen see a future for himself as a Welsh national poet? There are fragments of *Perseus* in the British Museum; they are exceedingly obscure but they contain some familiar subject matter, including a descent into Hell, and seem to be parts of a narrative in blank verse. *Idylls in Prose* remain unexplained. Owen might well have tried his hand at prose after the war: he enjoyed writing humorous pieces for *The Hydra* and at Craiglockhart drafted a facetious anti-war play called *Two Thousand* (about the federation of Europe and America in that year).

Robert Graves told Owen that after the war he must help 'S.S. and R.N. and R.G. to revolutionize English Poetry'. Although all three survived the war, neither Sassoon nor Nichols nor Graves himself turned out to be literary revolutionaries. It may be that Owen would have joined the movement to revive verse drama; certainly his admiration for Yeats would have remained, and perhaps Yeats would have learned to admire Owen in return. On the other hand, neither *Perseus* nor any late unpublished work (some of which is remarkably bad) gives much promise that Owen would have taken an immediate lead in any 'revolution'. It is hard indeed to believe that the zeal of *Strange Meeting* and the original genius of *Spring Offensive* could have dwindled away in peacetime. Such speculation, however, is idle: from the first, Owen's work was prophetic of his early death.

B. THE MANUSCRIPTS

It is sometimes believed of Owen that he scribbled his poems out in the trenches on any paper that was available and never had time to revise them. Nothing could be further from the truth. Almost all his published poems exist as careful fair copies in the British Museum collection. The editor's problem is not to reconstruct poems from inadequate fragments but to decide which of perhaps half a dozen careful revisions is the one which Owen intended as final. There are some cases, however, where Owen wrote the fair copy and then made very hasty alterations to it later; *S.I.W.*, for example, is so heavily altered that it is beyond certain reading in places. It is very unusual, of course, for a modern poet to die before seeing his work into print; Owen's manuscripts are thus particularly interesting documents.

An appreciable number of manuscripts remain in private hands, but many are drafts of published poems. Mrs Owen appears to have given some manuscripts to her friends; it may be that there is more of Owen's work preserved than has yet come to light, but we cannot hope for much.

Most of the unpublished poems are either in the British Museum or among the papers of the late Harold Owen. It was always Mr Owen's hope that a complete edition would one day be produced, but he was not in favour of piecemeal publication and consistently refused permission for quotation to be made from any unpublished MSS. On the whole, this ruling (which remains in force) has been a good thing; Owen's reputation has been able to establish itself on the basis of his comparatively few mature poems and the critic has not had to plough through quantities of juvenilia. Apart from a few set pieces, competently done, such as a long verse rendering of Hans Andersen's *The Little Mermaid* and a number of sonnets (about a quarter of all Owen's poems are sonnets), the unpublished material is mainly interesting for the insights which it gives into Owen's personality and development. There are fragments which suggest, for example, that he suffered from violent dreams long before 1917.

On this and similar questions, such as his possible homosexuality, it seems sensible not to speculate until the full biographical facts are known.

There are, of course, many unpublished drafts of the war poems, but at least one draft of every war poem known to me is in the 1963 edition, with the exception of *An Imperial Elegy* (? 1916) and *The Ballad of Purchase Money* (? 1915, later revised under other titles). These two poems have unfortunately only been published in part. In the *Ballad*, death in war is described as *sweeter still and far more meet* than life in peacetime; the *Elegy*, subtitled *Libretto for Marche Funebre*, is a funeral march in words in which the trenches are seen from above as not *one corner of a foreign field* but *the Path of Glory* spanning Europe. This attempt to outdo Rupert Brooke is unfinished; it can be compared with *The Show*, and the *Ballad* with *Dulce et Decorum Est*. Owen's hatred of war did not begin until 1917.

One disadvantage of Mr Harold Owen's rule is that it is not yet possible to make more than slight emendations to the 1963 text. In some cases of doubt, the 1963 edition seems to have followed the 1931 text rather than the MSS, preserving various 'conflations' of different drafts (as in *Conscious*, *The Next War* and *Asleep*) which do not correspond to any single MS; accepting without comment a number of reconstructions from cancelled workings (such as the opening lines of *From My Diary*); and in at least one instance, *The Chances*, reproducing what is almost certainly not Owen's final draft. I have, however, been able to restore some of what I believe to be Owen's original punctuation and lineation; most of these changes are not significant enough to be mentioned in the Notes, but I hope that where the present text differs from its predecessors it does so on sound MS authority.

THE MAKING OF
ANTHEM FOR DOOMED YOUTH

The material in this appendix shows the growth of one poem. Notes are kept to a minimum.

(i)

To a Comrade in Flanders

Seeing we never spied frail Fairyland,
    Though small we crouched by bluebells, moon by moon,
And are too late for Lethe's tide; too soon
    For that new bridge that leaves old Styx half-spanned:
5 Nor meekly unto Mecca caravanned;
    Nor bugled Asgard, skilled in magic rune;
Nor yearned for far Nirvana, the sweet swoon;
    And are from Paradise cursed out and banned:

Let's die back to those hearths we died for. Thus
10 Shall we be gods there. Death shall be no sev'rance.
In dull, dim chancels, flower new shrines for us.
For us, rough knees of boys shall ache with rev'rance;
For girls' breasts are the clear white Acropole
Where our own mothers' tears shall heal us whole.

This sonnet (dated *Sept. 1916*) may well have been one of those which WO asked his mother to send him urgently after his first meeting with SS. The ideas in it would thus have been fresh in his mind when he came to write *Anthem* a few days later. There are four drafts, one entitled *A New Heaven/To — on Active Service*.

[All sounds have been as music : a fragment]

All sounds have been as music to my listening:
  Pacific lamentations of slow bells,
The crunch of boots on blue snow rosy-glistening,
  Shuffle of autumn leaves; and all farewells.

5 Bugles that sadden all the evening air,
  And country bells clamouring their last appeals
Before [the] music of the evening prayer;
  Bridges, sonorous under carriage wheels.

Gurgle of sluicing surge through hollow rocks,
10 The gluttonous lapping of the waves on weeds,
Whisper of grass; the myriad-tinkling flocks,
  The warbling drawl of flutes and shepherds' reeds.

The orchestral noises of October nights
  Blowing [   ] symphonetic storms
15 Of startled clarions [   ]
  Drums, rumbling and rolling thunderous and [ ].

Thrilling of throstles in the keen blue dawn,
  Bees fumbling and fuming over sainfoin-fields

[Bugles sang : a fragment]

Bugles sang, saddening the evening air,
And bugles answered, sorrowful to hear.

Voices of boys were by the river-side.
Sleep mothered them; and left the twilight sad.

5 The shadow of the morrow weighed on men
[morn]

Voices of old despondency resigned
[Bowed] by the shadow of the morrow, slept.

[   ]dying tone
10 Of receding voices that will not return.

The wailing of the high far-travelling shells
And the deep cursing of the [   ].

The monstrous anger of our taciturn guns.
The majesty of the insults of their mouths.

Neither fragment is titled or dated. *Bugles sang* is a selection made by EB from a page of very fragmentary attempts at a series of pararhymed couplets. *All sounds* is more finished but it peters out for obvious reasons. The fragments contain material for both *Anthem* and *Disabled* and are likely, therefore, to have been written at Craiglockhart. With *All sounds*, compare the opening of SS's *Alone*:

> I've listened: and all sounds I heard
> Were music,—wind and stream and bird.

(iii)

The final version of *Anthem* was completed by 25th September 1917, when WO sent it home with the comment that SS had supplied the word 'Anthem' ('just what I meant it to be'). There are no fewer than seven surviving drafts and at least two part-drafts; the four given here are in BM and photographs of them are given by CDL in his third Appendix. They have been simplified in places. Words in italics and cancellations in dotted lines are pencilled suggestions made by SS when WO showed the drafts to him at Craiglockhart.

Drawing down the blinds of a house, now an almost forgotten custom, indicated either that a funeral procession was passing or that there had been a death in the house. It was customary to keep the coffin in the house until taking it to church; it would be placed in the darkened parlour, with a pall and flowers on it and lighted candles nearby. Relatives and friends would enter the room to pay their last respects. The sestet of the poem, in fact, refers to a household in mourning.

Anthem for Dead Youth

passing
What ~~minute~~-bells for these who die so fast?

      { *solemn*   *the*
—Only the { monstrous anger of ~~our~~ guns.

blind insolence   *iron*
Let the ~~majestic insults~~ of ~~their iron~~ mouths

            requiem   *requiem*
Be as the ~~priest-words~~ of their ~~burials.~~

Leave   *organs for the old*
5 ~~Of~~ choristers and holy music, none;

      Nor any voice of mourning, save the wail

And the   *hiss*   *lonely*
~~The~~ long-~~drawn wail~~ of ~~high~~ far-sailing shells.

            to light
What candles may we hold ~~for~~ these lost? ~~souls?~~

—Not in the hands of boys, but in their eyes,

      shine the   ~~tapers~~   the holy ~~tapers~~   candles
10   Shall ⋀ many ~~candles; shine; and [? I] will light them~~
              ~~holy~~ flames: to

And   Women's wide-~~spreaded~~ arms shall be their wreaths,

    And pallor of girls' cheeks shall be their palls.

            ~~mortal~~
Their flowers, the tenderness of ~~all men's~~ minds,
            ~~comrades'~~
            rough men's

     each slow
And ~~every~~ Dusk, a drawing-down of blinds.

for

Anthem ~~to~~ Dead Youth

What passing-bells for you who die in herds?

the

—Only the monstrous anger of ~~more~~ guns!

—Only the stuttering rifles' rattled words

Can patter out your hasty orisons.

choirs

5 No chants for you, nor balms, nor wreaths, nor bells

Nor any voice of mourning, save the choirs,

shells

And long-drawn sighs

~~The shrill demented choirs~~ of wailing shells;

And bugles calling for you from sad shires.

What candles may we hold to speed you all?

10 Not in the hands of boys, but in their eyes

Shall s   ~~and gleams~~ our

~~Shall~~ Shine the holy lights ∧ of ~~long~~ goodbyes.

must

The pallor of girls' brows ~~shall~~ be your pall;

comrades'

~~broken simple frail mortal~~

Your flowers, the tenderness of ~~mortal~~ minds,

~~pain-white~~

~~grief-wh~~ ~~innocent~~

And each slow dusk, a drawing-down of blinds.

THIRD DRAFT

What passing-bells for these ~~po~~ dumb-dying cattle?

—Only the monstrous anger of more guns!

Only the stuttering rifles' rapid rattle

Can patter out their hasty orisons.

5 No chants for them, nor wreaths, nor asphodels,
    Nor any voice of mourning save the choirs
The shrill demented choirs of wailing shells;
    And bugles calling for them from sad shires.

What candles may we hold to speed them all?
10   Not in the hands of boys, but in their eyes
Shall shine the holy gleams of their goodbyes.
    The pallor of girls' cheeks shall be their pall.
Their flowers the tenderness of silent minds
And each slow dusk a drawing-down of blinds.

FOURTH DRAFT

Doomed
Anthem for ~~Dead~~ Youth

What passing bells for these who die as cattle?

—Only the monstrous anger of the guns.

Only the stuttering rifles' rapid rattle

Can patter out their hasty orisons.

      { ~~music for all them~~ ~~nor~~ *no*   nor
5 No { mockeries for them; ~~from~~ prayers ~~or~~ bells
          now

Nor any voice of mourning save the choirs,
           ented
The shrill ~~demonic~~ choirs of wailing shells;
     ~~disconsolate~~

And bugles calling ~~sad across the~~ shires.
          for them from sad

What candles may be held to speed them all?
10   Not in the hands of boys, but in their eyes

Shall shine the holy glimmers of goodbyes.

~~And~~ The pallor of girls' brows shall be their pall;

                    { ~~silent~~ *patient*
Their flowers the tenderness of { ~~sweet white~~ minds,
And each slow dusk a drawing-down of blinds.

150

APPENDIX IV
BIBLIOGRAPHY

Apart from the works of Keats and Shelley, perhaps the most important single piece of background reading to Owen is the wartime poetry of Siegfried Sassoon. This appeared in two volumes in Owen's lifetime, *The Old Huntsman* (1917) and *Counter-Attack* (1918), both of which are included in Sassoon's *Collected Poems* (1947, but recently reprinted). Owen also showed much enthusiasm for Robert Graves's *Fairies and Fusiliers* (1917); Mr Graves has since withdrawn his war poetry but some of it will be found in anthologies.

Owen recorded his life pretty fully in his many letters; almost all have been preserved and are published in *Wilfred Owen: The Collected Letters*, edited by Harold Owen and John Bell (1967). There is a full and usually reliable index. Mr Harold Owen also recorded a detailed portrait of his brother in the three volumes of *Journey from Obscurity: Wilfred Owen 1893-1918, Memoirs of the Owen Family* (1963-65)—volumes which are fascinating reading in their own right, though there is an abridged version edited for schools by E. M. Gornall. In 1970, Mr Owen completed *Aftermath*, the sequel to his trilogy. All his books are published by the Oxford University Press.

There are few reminiscences of Owen by people who knew him: Sassoon wrote an important chapter on him in *Siegfried's Journey 1916-1920* (1945) and Osbert Sitwell devoted one to him in *Noble Essences* (1950). Further recollections, together with some criticism, will be found in *A Tribute to Wilfred Owen*, a booklet compiled by T. J. Walsh to mark the opening in 1964 of the Birkenhead Institute's Wilfred Owen Memorial Library.

All the editions of Wilfred Owen's poems have been published by Chatto and Windus. The first edition was by Sassoon, though most of the work seems to have been done by Edith Sitwell; it appeared in 1920, and contained twenty-three poems. Edmund Blunden's edition (1931) contained fifty-nine poems, some notes and a Memoir. C. Day Lewis edited the 'definitive' *Collected Poems* in 1963; he included eighty poems and much information about the text and variant readings, but the collection is not, of course, complete.

The accuracy of the 1963 text owed much to the scholarship of Professor D. S. R. Welland, whose *Wilfred Owen: A Critical Study* (1960) remains the only monograph on Owen to have appeared in England. A recent American publication—*Wilfred Owen* by Gertrude M. White (1969)—is useful but breaks little new ground.

The following books are some of those which have sections on Owen:

Bergonzi, Bernard. *Heroes' Twilight: A Study of the Literature of the Great War* (1965)

Grubb, Frederick. *A Vision of Reality: A Study in Liberalism in Twentieth Century Verse* (1965)

Johnston, John H. *English Poetry of the First World War: A Study in the Evolution of Lyric and Narrative Form* (1964)

Silkin, Jon. *Out of Battle: the Poetry of the Great War* (1972)

Thwaite, Anthony. *Contemporary English Poetry: An Introduction* (1959)

Articles about Owen in periodicals are legion, though few of them offer original criticism of direct interest to the average reader; many are in American publications and not easily available in England. An almost complete list is given in William White's *Wilfred Owen (1893-1918): A Bibliography* (Kent State University Press, 1965), to which the specialist is referred. The most adventurous critic of Owen in America has so far been Professor Joseph Cohen; his articles are worth reading, although one must have serious reservations about some of his conclusions and most of his methods. In England, the list of writers about the 'poet's poet' includes such names as Dylan Thomas, D. J. Enright, Ted Hughes, Louis MacNeice, Philip Larkin and Patric Dickinson; his three editors and many of his early defenders were poets also. Academic criticism, however, has been sparse; and it has tended to be more concerned with charting the growth of Owen's reputation than with the poems themselves.

The First World War produced a remarkable quantity of good poetry and a number of very fine prose works. This is a body of literature worth reading in itself but it also forms excellent background material to a reading of Owen. The list below contains the two best anthologies and some outstanding memoirs and novels (the

last two are by Germans). A much larger list is given in *Heroes'*
Twilight.

Gardner, Brian (ed.). *Up the Line to Death: The War Poets, 1914-
1918* (1964)

Parsons, I. M. (ed.). *Men who March Away: Poems of the First
World War* (1965)

Aldington, Richard. *Death of a Hero* (1929)

Barbusse, Henri. *Under Fire* (1917)

Blunden, Edmund. *Undertones of War* (1928)

Graves, Robert. *Goodbye to All That* (1929)

Hemingway, Ernest. *A Farewell to Arms* (1929)

Read, Herbert. *In Retreat* (1925)

Sassoon, Siegfried. *The Complete Memoirs of George Sherston* (1937)

Jünger, Ernst. *The Storm of Steel* (1929)

Remarque, E. M. *All Quiet on the Western Front* (1929)

INDEX OF FIRST LINES
AND TITLES